AMERICAN ADVENTURES

True Stories From America's Past
1770 – 1870
Part 1

By
Morrie Greenberg

Former English-Social Studies Consultant,
Los Angeles Unified School District

Brooke-Richards Press
Northridge, California

OTHER BOOKS BY MORRIE GREENBERG

The Buck Stops Here, A Biography of Harry Truman, **Macmillan**

We the People **(multi-state history text adoptions, including California), D.C. Health**

Adventures in United States History **(Federal Grant)**

Survival in the Square, **Brooke-Richards Press**

American Adventures, Part 2, 1870 to Present, **Brooke-Richards Press**

American Heroes, 1735-1900 **Brooke-Richards Press**

Published by
Brooke-Richards Press
9420 Reseda Blvd., # 511
Northridge, California 91324

Printed in the United States of America
Ninth Printing, 2005

ISBN 0-9622652-1-7

Library of Congress Cataloging-in Publication Data
Greenberg, Morrie.
  American adventures : true stories from America's past / by Morrie Greenberg.
    p. cm.
  Contents: pt 1. 1770–1870.
  Summary: Summary: A kaleidoscope of fifteen stories about United States history.
  1. United States—History—Anecdotes—Juvenile literature.
[1. United States—History.] I. Title.
E178.3.G82   1991
973—dc20
                                          90-2652
                                          CIP
                                          AC

Contents

Acknowledgments

The author wishes to acknowledge the fine input provided by these teachers: Matthew Cruz, Diane Goldstein, Dr. Helen Lodge, John Plevack, George Rollins, Sue Shapiro, and Ron Sima.

Book design by Suzette Mahr. Cover design and illustration by Laurel Long. Production assistance, Rand Self. Editor, Audrey Bricker.

About the Author

Morrie Greenberg has served as a teacher, a department chairperson, an administrative consultant, and a school principal. As English-Social Studies consultant for the Los Angeles Unified School District, he worked with, and offered suggestions to, teachers at thirty different schools. He also taught Methods of Teaching Social Studies at California State University, Northridge, and coordinated a tutoring program for teenagers there. He is presently supervising teachers at CSUN.

To The Reader

This is a book of stories that other young readers and listeners have found interesting and exciting. We hope you will too.

To the left of each story is a timeline and a box titled, "What Else Was Happening?" This will give you an idea of what was happening at about the time the story is taking place. Since the stories and timelines follow in order, you will get a chance to see how our nation has grown.

Though the stories in *American Adventures* happened long ago, you will discover that many people and events in the stories remind you of what is happening today. A writer in ancient Rome had something to say about this over 2,000 years ago. He wrote:

**Why do you laugh? Change but
the name and the story is told of you.**

1781

1770 — Angry colonists riot against British soldiers in Boston

1773 — Colonists protest tax on tea, hold "Boston Tea Party"

1775 — Patrick Henry speaks out against British rule: "Give me liberty, or give me death"

1775 — Minute Men fire on British at Lexington and Concord

1776 — (July 4) Colonists declare their independence from Great Britain. War for Independence begins

1781 — British surrender at Yorktown. War for Independence won.

1781 — Families from Mexico start settlement in California

What Else Was Happening?

The colonists who lived in the thirteen English colonies during the late 1700's wanted to be able to rule their own colonies. The British Parliament in England, however, kept passing laws that took away many of their rights and freedoms. Angered by this, the colonists declared their independence from Great Britain on July 4, 1776, and the War for Independence began. General George Washington was placed in command of the colonial army. After five years of fighting, the colonists won their independence from England. In 1781 a new nation, the United States, was born. Meantime, Mexico to the south, remained in the Spanish empire.

#1
Moving North

Maria Variegas breathed a deep sigh of relief as she halted along the gentle slope that led toward the river. The river was but a trickle now, but Maria knew that the winter rains would fill it with the water they would need to irrigate the land. *Farming would be good!*

Maria and her husband, Jose, walked along the dusty Indian trail to the shade of some willow branches. The other settlers—all on foot—followed. *At last, they were here!* What a long, exhausting journey it had been. The Spanish officials had told them the journey would be difficult, but back in Mexico, neither Maria nor Jose could have imagined just how rough a journey it would be.

Twelve Mexican families—23 men and women and 21 children—had left the town of Alamos, Mexico, on February 2, 1781, to settle in Upper California. There was but one other settlement in all of Upper California. At this time Mexico, including Upper California (as California was then called), belonged to Spain. The families had walked the 100 miles from Alamos to the western coast of Mexico. Here they boarded a small, rickety boat that sailed across the Gulf of California and landed them on a shore in Lower California.

The first signs of the "sickness" came shortly after the landing. Small, red markings began to show on the faces of some of the children. The marks grew larger, then spread to their arms and legs. Within a few days, the marks turned to blisters and chills racked the children's fevered bodies. *Small pox!* Maria and the other parents had stayed awake night after night hovering over the sick children.

Somehow, the children survived, and the families pushed on. They moved northward, encircling huge boulders where there were no trails, or cutting across rocky paths that left their feet bloody and sore. On they moved, always north, across desolate deserts, and over rugged mountains.

Meantime, a group of Spanish soldiers were moving most of the families' livestock along a different route—northward to Arizona, and then west to California. They had taken this longer, more treacherous route because there were too many animals to load onto the boat. The settlers knew that the soldiers would have to herd the goats, horses, cows, mules, and cattle across the Sonora and Mojave deserts. They prayed for their safe arrival.

Four months after they had begun the journey, exhausted, yet filled with hope, Maria and Jose and the other settlers had arrived at the San Gabriel mission. The mission was a few miles from where they hoped to settle.

Maria picked up a handful of soil near the river and let it slide through her fingers. She had never really wanted to leave their home and friends in Mexico and move to Upper California. Then, one day, two Spanish offi-

Courtesy, Seaver Center for Western History Research,
L.A. County Museum of Natural History

At last, they were here!

cials visited her town. Spain was anxious to start settlements in California to stop other countries from claiming it. The officials told the people of the town that they were looking for good farmers—and their families—who knew how to irrigate a plot of land, and who were willing to work very hard.

Maria and Jose had listened carefully that day. Each family would receive a plot of land large enough to build a home, and two large fields for growing crops. Each family would also receive two cows, two goats, two horses, three mares and a mule. Maria and Jose had heard enough. They told the Spanish officials they would go.

As the weeks passed, Maria and the other settlers marked out their plots of land, worked on their fields, and waited patiently for word about the soldiers and the livestock. One day a messenger arrived. The settlers greeted him warmly, but the news he brought saddened them greatly.

The soldiers had moved the livestock as far as the Colorado River. When nearby Indians discovered that the animals were trampling over and eating the vegetation, they grew very angry. They depended on the land for their food. Fearful that they would starve, the Indians attacked the soldiers and slaughtered the animals.

The news stunned Maria and the other settlers. Some of the settlers felt crushed, but Maria knew they had to keep working and building. The settlers were all experienced farmers. Some of them were carpenters and masons. There was even a tailor, and a skilled blacksmith. They set to work building homes, laying out irrigation ditches, and planting crops.

As Maria and Jose and the small band of settlers from Mexico worked on their settlement, they had no way of knowing about another group of settlers some three thousand miles to the east. In this same year, 1781, this other group of settlers, or colonists, were fighting for their independence from England.

Though the settlers of the thirteen colonies had come earlier, the two groups were alike in many ways. Alone, and with no chance of ever returning to their homes, they were willing to take on the unknown and to face any hardship—all for a chance to start a new life.

As the years passed, the children and grandchildren of Maria and Jose Variegas and the other settlers planted more crops, raised more animals, built more homes, and laid out roads. The settlement grew from a village to a town to a city. Along with many other traditions left by these early Mexican settlers, the city kept its Spanish name, "Queen of the Angels," or, Los Angeles.

Writing / Journal Activities

1. The Story

Write three important things that you learned from reading or listening to the story, "Moving North."

2. Find The Word

Copy the ONE WORD in each row that best describes the settlers in this story.

Read Across →

1. ignorant, persevering, weak

2. ambitious, frail, dull

3. hesitant, backward, determined

4. industrious, hopeless, lazy

3. Search and Find

Find the word (or words) closest to the meaning of the <u>underlined</u> word in each sentence. Then, copy the sentence, using that word (or words) in place of the underlined word.

1. The river was but a <u>trickle</u> now.
   thin stream   lake   pond   torrent

2. They would have to know how to <u>irrigate</u> the land.
   cultivate   water   plant   farm

3. They boarded a <u>rickety</u> boat and sailed across the gulf.
   shaky   sturdy   old   small

4. They had to cross a <u>desolate</u> land.
   dry   quiet   cold   deserted

5. The soldiers took a route that was even more <u>treacherous</u>.
   out of the way   deserted   overgrown   dangerous

6. Some of the settlers were <u>skilled</u> workers.
   old   untrained   capable   hard

Let's Talk – Discussion Activities

4. Think It Through

Give as many answers as you can for each question.

—Why do you think the Spanish officials wanted only farmers who had families to become settlers?

—Why do you think the Spanish officials wanted settlers as well as soldiers living in Upper California?

5. Take A Side

Here are two opinions on the same subject. Take one side or the other, and then give all the reasons you can for the side you take.

Is it a good idea to suffer and take on hardships for a chance at a better life?

—"Yes. Our country is great because so many people were willing to suffer and take chances."

—"No. It's better to wait for an easy way to better your life."

6. Then And Now

Compare the past with the present. Give as many answers as you can for each question.

—What are some of the hardships U.S. immigrants (people new to the U.S.) face today?

—How can an immigrant overcome some of these hardships?

Cooperative Group Activities

7. Imagine

Imagine that you are one of the settlers in the story on your way to California. Imagine that you keep a diary. Write about what happened to you on four different days.

8. A Look Back

Select one of the events shown on the timeline for this story. Use other books or articles to gather more information about the event, and try to find out why the event was important. Present the information to the class.

1799

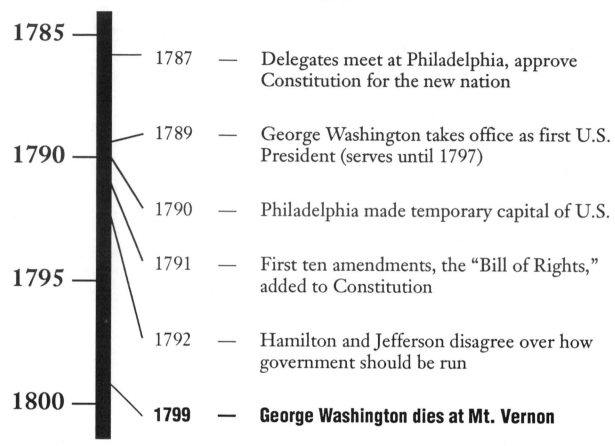

1785

1787 — Delegates meet at Philadelphia, approve Constitution for the new nation

1789 — George Washington takes office as first U.S. President (serves until 1797)

1790

1790 — Philadelphia made temporary capital of U.S.

1791 — First ten amendments, the "Bill of Rights," added to Constitution

1795

1792 — Hamilton and Jefferson disagree over how government should be run

1800

1799 — George Washington dies at Mt. Vernon

What Else Was Happening?

Though Americans called their new nation the "United States" in 1781, the country was weak and not united at all. The Articles of Confederation, an agreement between the states for running the country, was not working. In 1789 a new plan for running the country, called the Constitution, was approved. The new Constitution gave the central government more power and made the U.S. a stronger, more united nation. George Washington was elected the nation's first president. He served for eight years and his wise decisions and strong leadership gave the young country the good start it needed.

The "Good Old Days" of Medicine

George Washington tossed and turned in bed this cold December morning in 1799. Two days before, the retired President had ridden on horseback across Mt. Vernon through the bitter cold and snow, then returned home, tired and not feeling well. This morning the sixty-seven year old first President of the United States felt worse. Doctors were called. They had him gargle with a mixture of molasses, vinegar, and butter, and placed a paste of dried beetles across his throat. They took blood from the ailing President—not once, not twice, but four times.

Little wonder then that Washington was finally moved to say, "I pray you take no more trouble about me. Let me go quietly." He died December 14, 1799, at 10:00 p.m.

Today's doctors have many ways of helping patients and making them feel better, but this was not true in George Washington's time. In those days the treatment was supposed to hurt. Medicine was supposed to taste awful, and the patient was supposed to feel miserable. How else—so the doctor's thinking went—could the doctor drive "the sickness" out of the patient?

Americans of the late 1700's and early 1800's who placed themselves in the hands of doctors were in for some strange treatments. There were drugs vile enough to make patients stagger and forget who they were, and medicines that made patients froth at the mouth and vomit. In each case the doctor was quick to explain that the terrible taste and the strange reactions of the patients only proved that the medicine was doing its work.

Some doctors had other ideas for driving out "the sickness." Pity the helpless man or woman who had a doctor who believed that the best cure for an illness was to dunk the patient in freezing water until the patient turned blue. Or, the poor patient whose doctor believed that the cure was to place the patient in a steam bath hot enough to make the patient scream.

Doctors of those early days saved the worst treatment of all, however, for their sickest patients. If someone had a high fever, ached all over, or felt so weak he could not even make his way out of bed, the doctor solemnly announced that the patient had "bad blood." And everyone knew what to do about "bad blood"—it had to be taken out.

To remove the "bad blood," the doctor cut a vein in the patient's arm and proceeded to draw the blood out by squeezing on a small bulb. Sometimes, the doctor used leeches (a leech is a type of worm) instead of the bulb. Leeches were placed on the patient's chest, and left to suck out the "bad blood."

The men and women who moved westward in the late 1700's and early 1800's, depended on doctors who traveled from one place to another. More often than not, this traveling doctor had never attended a medical school. Instead, he stuffed his saddlebag with

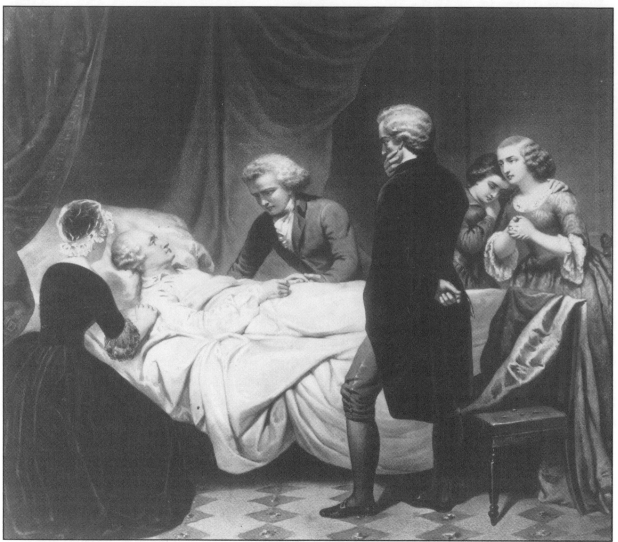

Courtesy, National Archives

Washington was moved to say, "Let me go quietly."

a few drugs and a knife, and simply announced he was a doctor. Little wonder then, that many pioneers brave enough to take on all hardships, kept their distance from the friendly doctor. These hardy pioneers turned to what has come to be called, "home remedies." We do not know for certain how most of these home remedy ideas began, but we do know that they were passed on from one person to another for many years.

Here are a few of the home remedies practiced by early pioneers of the West.

• If a baby is teething, tie some beads around the baby's neck.

• If someone has a toothache, pick the bad tooth with the splint of a tree that was struck by lightning.

• If someone has a fever, have the patient chew on turnip roots.

• To help someone with a bad cough, take a strip of raw pork and wrap it around the patient's neck. If this doe not work, take the skin of a dead fish and tie it to the patient's feet.

• To stop bleeding, place some spider-webs on the wound. If this does not work, try mud, coffee grounds, flour, spit, axle grease, or the inside of an eggshell.

• To heal a bruise, place boiled potato scrapings, or raw bacon on it.

• If someone has a burn, take some burned rabbit fur, beat it to a powder, add oil, and place it on the burn.

• If someone has a cold, have them drink honey mixed with boiled onions. Or try powdered dried frog skins, or pickle juice, or vinegar mixed with water. If none of these work, slice an onion and place it on a window sill.

• If someone has a stiff neck, have the person scratch his or her neck on a tree that was scratched by a hog.

• Stop a headache by having the patient lean his or her head against a tree. Then have another person hammer a nail into the other side of the tree. Other things to try: run around your house three times; stand on your head until you get dizzy; or tie the head of a buzzard around your neck.

• If someone is bitten by a snake, cut a chicken in half and place it on the bite. Keep it there until the chicken turns green.

• Relieve a sunburn by cutting a raw tomato and rubbing it over the burn.

Americans would have to wait until the middle and late 1800's before doctors began to use remedies based on science.

Writing / Journal Activities

1. The Story

Write three important things that you learned from reading or listening to the story, "The 'Good Old Days' of Medicine."

2. Find The Word

Copy the ONE WORD in each row that best describes a doctor of these early days.

Read Across →

1. harmful, dependable, old
2. healthy, reliable, damaging
3. helpful, uneducated, healing
4. perfect, hurtful, young

3. Search And Find

Find the word (or words) closest to the meaning of the underlined word in each sentence. Then, copy the sentence, using that word (or words) in place of the underlined word.

1. They took blood from the ailing President.
   tired   sick   weak   old

2. Americans were in for some strange treatments.
   remedies   warnings   illnesses   diseases

3. There were drugs vile enough to make patients forget who they were.
   sweet   sour   good   disgusting

4. The doctors explained that the strange reactions proved that the medicine worked.
   changes   spirits   sicknesses   colors

5. The doctor solemnly announced that the patient had bad blood.
   carefully   seriously   coldly   loudly

6. The hardy pioneers turned to home remedies.
   frightened   old   ill   strong

Let's Talk – Discussion Activities

4. Think It Through

Give as many answers as you can for each question.

—Why do you think people in these early days were afraid of doctors?

—Why do you think so many people in these early days believed in strange cures?

5. Take A Side

Here are two opinions on the same subject. Take one side or the other, and then give all the reasons you can for the side you take.

Is it important to study the past?

—"Yes, it's important to learn about what happened hundreds of years ago."

—"No, it's a waste of time to learn about what happened hundreds of years ago."

6. Then And Now

Compare the past with the present. Give as many answers as you can for each question.

—Why do these early cures sound so silly to us today?

—Will some of our beliefs or cures sound silly to people a hundred years from now? Can you guess which of today's beliefs might prove to be wrong?

Cooperative Group Activities

7. Imagine

Imagine that you are a radio or television talk show doctor living in the early 1800's. Prepare and present a program where a number of people phone in with different ailments. As the doctor, present a remedy for each call.

8. A Look Back

Select one of the events shown on the timeline for this story. Use other books or articles to gather more information about the event, and try to find out why the event was important. Present the information to the class.

1800

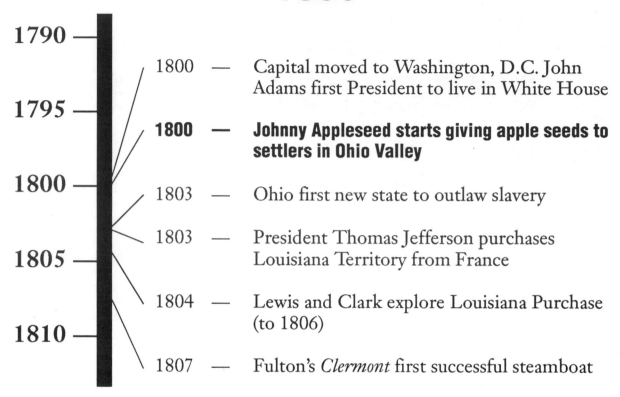

1790

1795

1800

1805

1810

1800 — Capital moved to Washington, D.C. John Adams first President to live in White House

1800 — Johnny Appleseed starts giving apple seeds to settlers in Ohio Valley

1803 — Ohio first new state to outlaw slavery

1803 — President Thomas Jefferson purchases Louisiana Territory from France

1804 — Lewis and Clark explore Louisiana Purchase (to 1806)

1807 — Fulton's *Clermont* first successful steamboat

What Else Was Happening?

America's pioneers had pushed westward, carving out new trails even before the War for Independence. By 1801 trailblazers had moved America's frontier as far west as the Mississippi River. Settlers followed the trailblazing pioneers in search of fertile land and a better place to raise their families. These hardy men and women cleared the land, then planted crops and harvested them. Their hard work changed the wilderness into a prosperous land.

In 1803 President Thomas Jefferson purchased the Louisiana Territory from France for a little more than fifteen million dollars. A huge new area now lay open for Americans to settle. In time this rich land of 828 thousand square miles would make up all or part of fifteen new states.

#3
Johnny Appleseed, Hero of the Wilderness

Anyone looking for a hero would have looked right past John Chapman. He had a funny looking beard that wandered about in all directions like a worn out old toothbrush, and—except for two cheek bones that stuck out like smooth rocks—his face was narrow and drawn in. He rarely wore shoes, but he did have an old burlap coffee sack to cover his thin frame. The sack had two holes for his arms, and a hole for his head. And, always—rain or shine—John wore a pair of old, patched up hand-me-down trousers.

Make a hero out of John Chapman? Like George Washington? or John Paul Jones? or Andrew Jackson? That did not make much sense.

John Chapman was born in Massachusetts in 1774. By the time John was twenty, he knew that he would never be happy if he had to stay in the same place all the time. And so, John began to wander. He roamed across the frontiers of Pennsylvania, Ohio, Indiana, and as far west as Illinois. There are towns and cities there now, but most of the country was wilderness then—and that was the way John liked it. He wandered everywhere—across grassy plains, over rolling hills, and through thick forests. Whenever night came, no matter where he was, John just made himself comfortable and bedded down for the night.

The pioneers of these early days trapped and hunted rabbits, beavers, weasels, deer—even bear. They cooked and ate the meat of these animals, and used their skins and furs to make clothes and to trade. John Chapman was different. No matter where he was, or how hungry he might be, he never hurt or killed a single animal.

"I can't kill something I love," John said. Even if someone else killed the animal, John refused to eat meat. Instead, he lived off of the fruits and berries he found in the wilderness. "I don't need to wear skins or fur either," he laughed. "This coffee sack is good enough for me." Once in a while, when the trail got pretty bad, he would break down and wear a pair of old shoes a farmer had given him. If a rattlesnake crossed his trail, or if an insect got in the way, or a startled rabbit scurried past, John always made sure to steer clear. These were "God's creatures" he said, and he did not wish to harm any of them.

Once John traded supplies for an old but sturdy horse. He put his belongings on the horse, and began walking alongside the animal. The farmer who had traded the horse watched in surprise.

"Why aren't you riding that critter?" he asked.

John was quick with his answer: "A horse deserves more dignity than that."

The farmer protested that everyone rode horses, and that John would not hurt the horse if he mounted it.

"Well, I may not hurt him so you can see it," John answered, "but if I got on him, it

Courtesy, The Bettmann Archive

Anyone looking for a hero would have looked right past John Chapman. (Drawing by a college student who had seen Johnny Appleseed)

might just hurt his pride."

In the early 1800's pioneers kept moving west. Often they pushed the Indians aside to make room for their farms and settlements. If the Indians fought back, there were bitter struggles. John Chapman was different. He had no thoughts of taking land or fighting the Indians. After all, the Indians were his friends.

A frontiersman who did not trap animals or pack a rifle or ride a horse or fight the Indians? Hardly the stuff frontier heroes are made of.

As John Chapman wandered through different parts of the Ohio Valley in the early 1800's, he knew that before too long other people would be coming to settle on the land. So, he would clear away a few acres and plant some apple seeds. By the time the settlers arrived, John had small apple trees all ready for them. He rarely sold the trees. Instead, he traded them for supplies such as salt, flour, potatoes, and corn meal. "Just give me enough to keep me going," he often told a new settler.

Sometimes a settler was too poor to pay John. That was all right too. A pleasant word was payment enough for John. And, next time he passed, why the settler might offer John a place to stay for a few nights—and that was payment too.

And so, John wandered up and down the Ohio River Valley—always with packs of apple seeds—planting as he went. Soon, the word spread about John. He was welcome wherever he chose to stay, but he never stayed in one place too long. And when he decided to be on his way, the settlers offered him warm good-byes, knowing, like as not, he would wander back come spring or fall. Sometimes he would do his planting near an Indian village. He was welcome there too, and it was from the Indians that he learned about herbs that could be used as medicines.

Soon, settlers in different parts of the Ohio River Valley began to look forward to his return. He always had stories to tell, herbal medicines to give, and "fun talk" for the children. He could quote from the Bible too. There was just something about John Chapman that made the settlers—young and old—feel good. No one knows just when, but before too long, the settlers got to calling John Chapman by another name: *Johnny Appleseed.*

"Here comes Johnny Appleseed!" the first child to see him would shout as he neared a town or settlement. Soon other children rushed toward him, and there would be a chorus of shouting: "Johnny Appleseed! Johnny Appleseed!" John was proud of the name. Apples were very valuable on the frontier.

The settlers used apple vinegar to pickle beans or cucumbers. They spread apple butter on their bread. They drank apple brandy and ate apple pie. And, best of all, apples could be stored in a cold place for many months.

Johnny Appleseed was almost 74 years old when he died in 1847. Everyone had a "Johnny Appleseed" story to tell—how he stayed and helped a sick old man, how he recited long passages from the Bible, how he wouldn't kill the smallest bug, how "strange" his clothes were, how good he was to the children, how he made you laugh and feel good. And, always, how he carried packs of apple seeds for planting.

The stories spread to different parts of the country. Americans talked about Johnny Appleseed as though he were, well, some kind of hero, like Molly Pitcher in the War for Independence. Maybe he did not look like one, or act like one, but to the settlers who knew the kind wanderer who planted apple seeds, Johnny Appleseed was a real hero.

Writing / Journal Activities

1. The Story

Write three important things that you learned from reading or listening to the story, "Johnny Appleseed, Hero of the Wilderness."

2. Find The Word

Copy the ONE WORD in each row that best describes Johnny Appleseed.

Read Across →

1. caring, mean, lucky

2. powerful, stubborn, helpful

3. generous, loyal, bothersome

4. reckless, neat, independent

3. Search and Find

Find the word (or words) closest to the meaning of the underlined word in each sentence. Then, copy the sentence, using that word (or words) in place of the underlined word.

1. Johnny Appleseed <u>roamed</u> across the frontier.
   wandered   hurried   ran   scampered

2. Most of the country was a <u>wilderness</u>.
   a rainy land   an unsettled land   a dry land   a cold land

3. A <u>startled</u> rabbit scurried past.
   quick   surprised   wild   injured

4. Johnny Appleseed once traded supplies for an old but <u>sturdy</u> horse.
   beautiful   sure-footed   strong   majestic

5. Johnny Appleseed learned about <u>herbs</u> from the Indians.
   strange flowers   plants used as medicine
   bushes for food   trees used for building

6. Johnny Appleseed could <u>quote</u> from the Bible too.
   read   write   tell stories   repeat word for word

Let's Talk – Discussion Activities

4. Think It Through

Give as many answers as you can for each question.

—Why do you think most of the settlers liked Johnny Appleseed?

—Why do you think early settlers were so willing to help each other?

5. Take A Side

Here are two opinions on the same subject. Take one side or the other. Give all the reasons you can for the side you take.

Should we admire Johnny Appleseed?

—"We should admire Johnny Appleseed. He did many wonderful things."

—"Johnny Appleseed did so many silly things. We should not admire him."

6. Then And Now

Compare the past with the present. Give as many answers as you can.

—A person who does not behave the way most people do is sometimes called an "eccentric" person. Name some famous "eccentric" people living today. Tell how they are different.

Cooperative Group Activities

7. Imagine

Prepare and present a television program where you interview a number of settlers who knew Johnny Appleseed. Let your viewers find out what kind of person he was.

8. A Look Back

Select one of the events shown on the timeline for this story. Use other books or articles to gather more information about the event, and try to find out why the event was important. Present the information to the class.

1820

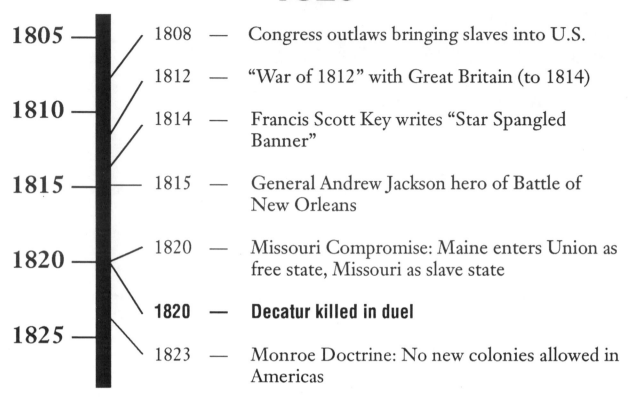

1805	
	1808 — Congress outlaws bringing slaves into U.S.
	1812 — "War of 1812" with Great Britain (to 1814)
1810	
	1814 — Francis Scott Key writes "Star Spangled Banner"
1815	1815 — General Andrew Jackson hero of Battle of New Orleans
	1820 — Missouri Compromise: Maine enters Union as free state, Missouri as slave state
1820	
	1820 — Decatur killed in duel
1825	
	1823 — Monroe Doctrine: No new colonies allowed in Americas

What Else Was Happening?

In 1807 British warships began pulling alongside American ships and taking off with some of the sailors on board. When the British kept ignoring America's demands to stop, the small, new nation decided this was more than it was willing to take. In 1812 the United States went to war with Great Britain.

The U.S. won a number of sea battles, but neither side really won the War of 1812. Because the U.S. had trouble getting manufactured goods during the war, Americans began making more things for themselves. By the time the war ended in 1814, the U.S. had built more factories than it ever had before.

#4

A Matter of Honor

Eight well dressed men stood bunched together on the small open field. They spoke in hushed tones, and cast nervous looks in all directions. The sun had not yet had a chance to burn away the early morning chill, and so a few of the men briskly rubbed their hands together. The morning light that slanted through the surrounding trees bathed the Maryland glen in yellow light—but the scene's beauty this March morning in 1820 gave no hint of the tragedy that was about to unfold.

One of the men gave a nervous hurried glance in all directions. He gripped a small stick in his right hand with which he now drew a single short line on the ground. Slowly, he march off eight paces, counting each pace aloud, then drew a second line.

"Gentleman, you may take your places."

Two figures, one in his early forties, the other a few years older, moved to the marks. Each figure carefully positioned his body sideways—and then turned to stare full faced at the other. Each gripped a pistol pointed downward. The man who had drawn the mark now looked to be certain that the onlookers were out of the way.

"You are to begin at the count of one," he began, "and you are to stop at the count of three. Do we all understand?"

Stephen Decatur stared coldly at his older opponent, James Barron. He watched Barron slowly raise his arm and aim his pistol towards him. Decatur gripped his own gun more firmly, raised it, and aimed at Barron's left hip. Standing straight as a rod, Decatur held his breath.

So, he thought, it had finally come to this—America's greatest Navy hero in a duel over a matter of honor...

Decatur became a midshipman in the U.S. Navy when he was only nineteen. He quickly rose through the ranks and gained a reputation as a capable and popular officer. When war broke out with Tripoli in 1804, he was placed in command of a two-masted warship. He led his crew in the capture of one enemy warship, and—in a daring move—he and his crew boarded another ship that they set ablaze. He returned to America a great hero.

Officer Joseph Barron had once served aboard a ship with Decatur, but fate had not been as kind to Barron. Before the War of 1812 broke out, Barron commanded an American warship that was shelled by a British man-of-war. Barron's ship—smaller and not in fighting shape—was no match for the British warship. Barron surrendered and let the British come aboard. Even though it was not wartime, Barron was court-martialed and told he could not command another American ship for five years. Disgraced, Barron left America for Europe.

He returned a few years after the War of 1812, and asked to command another Navy warship. Decatur—who had been one of the officers who had convicted him at the court-martial—spoke out against Barron. Barron was furious. *How could Decatur do this when the two men had once been shipmates?* When Barron's request to command another ship was turned down, Barron wrote Decatur a note accusing Decatur of stabbing him in the back.

Decatur stood firm—he called Barron a coward. A flurry of notes went back and forth. Barron accused Decatur of spreading lies and ugly rumors about him. Decatur accused Barron of waiting until the War of 1812 was over before asking to command a ship.

Barron grew more furious. He demanded an apology. Decatur answered that there was nothing to apologize for. Barron simmered. No matter how much he denied the charges, his fellow officer insisted that he was not worthy of taking command of a ship. Barron felt that his honor was so badly damaged by Decatur's remarks that there was only one answer…

Decatur gained a reputation as a capable and popular officer.

Now the two faced each other. There was the noise of someone clearing a throat. "Fire, One—"

The Maryland countryside echoed to the sounds of two pistol shots. Both men pitched forward, then slipped to the ground. The onlookers—the seconds and doctors—rushed towards the two crumbled figures. No one had to wonder if the bullets had found their marks. Spots of red were beginning to show on their clothing.

Within hours word would spread from the secret meeting place on the glen in Maryland to the capital in Washington, D.C., only a few miles away. Stephen Decatur, America's most honored naval sea captain, had suffered a serious wound in a duel with James Barron. Barron had also been wounded—in the leg—but he would recover. Decatur's wound was much more serious. He was moved to Washington D.C. where he died the next day.

Over the next few days Americans all over the capital wondered why. The answer was always the same. *It was, you see, "a matter of honor."* Americans had learned about the custom of dueling from soldiers and sailors visiting here from France, England, and Germany. In their countries, a man in the "upper class" who felt his honor was insulted could challenge someone to a duel.

It was not until after the War for Independence that dueling "caught on" in America. While there were some duels fought in Northern states, most of them took place in the South. Duels were the result of a real or imagined "insult." The "insult" usually involved what someone said about another man, or said about another man's family, or—worst of all—what someone said about a wife or girlfriend.

Once a man decided that he had been insulted, he wrote a note to the other party. In the note he told the other person how his honor had been damaged. He demanded an explanation or an apology. The other party then wrote back. He could say he was sorry and apologize, or he could stand by what he said—and await a challenge to a duel.

There were rules for dueling. Only men in the upper class could participate. No one in the upper class would stoop to dueling with a slave, or farmer, or common laborer. After all, nothing common people said could be considered an insult that would hurt someone's honor! (An "upper class" man might, instead, simply beat a common person with his cane.) On the other hand, if judges, doctors, lawyers, Congressmen, governors, newspaper publishers, wealthy planters, or high-ranking officers insulted one another, a challenge could be made.

Most Americans thought dueling was wrong. Laws were passed to stop the practice, but almost no one was ever charged with a crime for dueling. Men in the upper class argued that if they did nothing about an insult, they would lose too much face. In a way, one man was trapped into making the challenge, and the other man was trapped into accepting.

Andrew Jackson was one of the most famous Americans to fight in a duel—actually he probably fought in quite a few. One time Jackson challenged a man he accused of insulting Jackson's wife. During the duel, a bullet struck Jackson squarely in the chest. As blood gushed from the wound, he calmly took aim and fired. The bullet killed his opponent. Years after the duel, in 1829, Andrew Jackson became President of the United States.

By the time of the Civil War (1861 to 1865), dueling had died out. The reason seemed clear. Americans believed it was wrong. And besides, America was growing into a democratic nation—there simply was no room for an idea that depended on an "upper class."

Writing / Journal Activities

1. The Story

Write three important things that you learned from reading or listening to the story, "A Matter of Honor."

2. Find the Word

Copy the ONE WORD in each row that best describes Stephen Decatur.

Read Across →

1. brave, cowardly, dishonest

2. jolly, timid, adventurous

3. stubborn, weak, tired

4. sickly, daring, bragging

3. Search and Find

Find the word (or words) closest to the meaning of the underlined word in each sentence. Then copy the sentence, using the word (or words) in place of the underlined word.

1. They spoke in hushed tones.
   loud voices   angry voices   quiet voices   polite voices

2. He marched off eight paces.
   fence-posts   steps   feet   yards

3. Decatur and his crew boarded another ship that they set ablaze.
   attacked   captured   went onto   shot at

4. Barron demanded an apology.
   asked for   requested   begged for   insisted on

5. Americans learned about the custom of dueling from soldiers and sailors from Europe.
   rules   laws   tradition   regulations

6. America was becoming a democratic nation.
   a rich nation   an independent nation
   a nation of industries   a nation with equal rights

Let's Talk – Discussion Activities

4. Think It Through

Give as many answers as you can for each question.

—If you lived at this time, why would you want (or not want) Stephen Decatur as a friend?

—Why do you think most people believed that dueling was wrong?

5. Take A Side

Here are two opinions on the same subject. Take one side or the other, and then give all the reasons you can for the side you take.

Should there be laws to keep people from hurting themselves?

—"It is a good idea to have laws that keep people from hurting themselves. For example, there should be a law that makes a motorcycle driver wear a helmet."

—"If some people want to do something dangerous, that's their business. The law should leave them alone."

6. Then And Now

Compare the past with the present. Give as many answers as you can for each question.

—What are some stupid or silly things that people do today when they think they have been insulted?

—What can be done to stop people from doing these things?

Cooperative Group Activities

7. Imagine

Prepare and present a television program where you interview Stephen Decatur just before he steps out to duel with Joseph Barron. Ask him five or more questions.

8. A Look Back

Select one of the events shown on the timeline for this story. Use other books or articles to gather more information about the event, and try to find out why the event was important. Present the information to the class.

1829

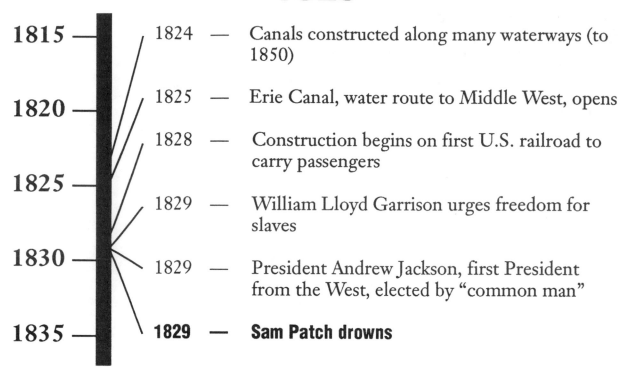

1815

1820

1825

1830

1835

1824 — Canals constructed along many waterways (to 1850)

1825 — Erie Canal, water route to Middle West, opens

1828 — Construction begins on first U.S. railroad to carry passengers

1829 — William Lloyd Garrison urges freedom for slaves

1829 — President Andrew Jackson, first President from the West, elected by "common man"

1829 — **Sam Patch drowns**

What Else Was Happening?

Americans and European immigrants who moved West found a whole new way of life. In the West a man was judged more on how hard he worked, how brave he was, or how willing he was to help his neighbor. Being rich or educated was less important. In the older, Eastern states only men who owned property and paid taxes could vote. As new Western states were added, these states gave most men the right to vote.

Andrew Jackson was the first President to come from the West and to be elected by the common man. Though rights for African Americans and women would not come until much later, Jackson's election was the beginning of a new kind of democracy. The common man could vote for the people who would run the government.

#5

Sam Patch – The Man Who Jumped to Fame

The old farmer who brought his two horses to a halt this frosty March morning in 1830 had no way of knowing the part he was about to play in solving a mystery—a mystery that had puzzled the people living in upstate New York for four months.

"Whoa," the farmer called pulling gently on the reins. The two horses clumped to a stop in the soft snow. As the farmer got out of the wagon his warm breath made white, steaming patterns on the cold air, and the horses snorted uncomfortably.

The farmer patted each of the horses. "Yes, we're gonna get you some water now," he said. He reached into the wagon and brought out an ax with a large wooden handle. He attacked the ice with hard, steady swings breaking it into small chunks. When he reached the frigid waters of the Genesee River below, he kept backing up and chipping away at the sides of the ice, making the circle of water larger. Suddenly something in the water caught his eye. What's that? The farmer let the ax slip into the snow. He got on his knees to get a better look.

"Oh, my," he whispered.

A soft sigh escaped the farmer's lips as he began to drag an object out of the water...

Ever since he was a small boy living in Rhode Island, Sam Patch liked to jump more than almost anything else in the world. Little Sam would walk to the middle of a bridge that spanned a river. Then—with friends and neighbors urging him on—Sam would let out with a yell, and jump straight into the water. Sometimes he jumped off a building next to some water or a cliff next to the river.

As Sam grew older, you would think that he would have outgrown his silly jumping habits. After all, jumping was for kids not a grown man. But jumping remained Sam's special love. "Jumping's just a lot of fun," Sam admitted.

When Sam was about twenty, he climbed on top of a bridge that spanned the Passaic Falls in New Jersey, looked down at the swirling waters seventy feet below, waved at a few friends down below—and jumped right in. A moment later he was swimming safely to shore.

A few months went by and Sam got another idea. He talked the owner of a large boat into building a wooden platform on top of the boat's masthead. With the boat anchored just outside of Hoboken, New Jersey, Sam climbed to the top of the platform. Now Sam looked down at the water a good 90 feet below. He had never jumped quite this far before. He took a deep breath and jumped overboard. When Sam burst to the surface a few moments later, he was greeted by sounds he had never heard before. Surprised and a little frightened, he made for the shore, but as he swam, the sounds grew louder and louder.

It wasn't until he reached the shore that Sam realized what was making the tremendous noise. People along the shore and in the surrounding boats were cheering—*cheering for him!* There must be hundreds of them, he thought—hundreds! Sam had never seen or heard anything like it before, but he did know one thing for sure—he liked it.

Sam had always picked when, where, and what would be "fun" to jump. Now Sam discovered things were going to be different. Newspapers picked up the story of *Sam Patch, The Jumping Man*, and how he had jumped of of the mast of a boat outside of Hoboken. People who read the stories would come from near and far just to see him jump. He would even get paid for letting them watch. What Sam did not know was that he was being pushed into a daring, dangerous game—a game he would have to keep on playing.

Months after the jump near Hoboken, posters in the town of Buffalo announced to one and all that on October 17, 1829, Sam Patch, The Jumping Man, would leap from an island that overlooked Niagara Falls, some 120 feet into the waters below. This death defying feat—the posters proclaimed—was a test of skill and daring that everyone would want to see.

There was a slow, steady rain on October 17, but a little wet weather was not going to stop Sam Patch. Thousands of spectators were on hand. Sam began to climb a ladder to a platform. The platform overlooking the Falls had been built atop four trees that had been tied together. As Sam climbed, people below cheered him on.

"Hooray for Sam, The Jumping Man."

"Come on, Sam, you can do it."

When Sam got to the top he walked around and strutted for ten minutes. By now, the people below were growing nervous. *Is he ever going to jump? Is he getting too scared? Will he get out alive?* Sam soon gave the audience an answer. He waved a right hand, kissed the large American flag that had been placed on the platform, took a deep breath, and—.

"There he goes!" someone shouted. Sam jumped straight down into the waters below.

A few moments later, Sam broke the surface, and cheer after cheer accompanied his swim to the rocky shoreline.

Ten weeks later, Sam Patch jumped off Genesee Falls with a pet bear. Both Sam and the bear survived. By now, Sam was big news—thousands of people were watching every jump he made, and thousands more were reading about him in the newspapers. Sam decided he would jump Genesee Falls again, but this time there would be a platform set up on the heights of the Falls so that he would be jumping from 125 feet.

"I want to set a new record," he told his friends.

People began to talk —about Sam, and how he was going to beat his old record. Before long, special coaches and boats were bringing people in from miles around—thousands of them—to watch Sam jump Genesee Falls. Nearby hotels filled up. It seemed as though everyone wanted to watch Sam break his record. *What a day it was going to be!*

Sam was not a diver—he was a jumper. To make the jump right, he had to jump feet first with his body rigid. He had to stay in this position, and land on the water feet first. That's why when Sam jumped from his platform this warm afternoon, the people in the crowed sensed something was wrong. Sam's arms and legs flailed at the air. He looked a little off-balance. He was trying to get his body in its usual upright position. Sam hit the water with a giant splash. The seconds past. A full minute went by. *Sam was nowhere in sight.*

Men were using ropes to drag the river now. They searched until darkness. Sam was gone. Now people talked about some things they remembered. *He seemed really nervous before the jump, didn't he?* And, he even told someone to be sure and give the four hundred dollar prize to his mother if he failed. "If he failed"—Sam never talked that way before.

Over the next few days, the newspapers

"There he goes!" someone shouted.

carried the story that Sam had drowned. But to the many people who had followed the career of Sam Patch, Sam was too good to let himself drown. He's just playing a trick on us, they said. *Why he found an underwater cave in the river before he jumped and left some dry clothes there. He just swam to that place, put on the clothes and sneaked away. Wait you'll see.* Other people claimed that Sam never jumped off the platform. *It was just a dummy made out of straw and rocks.* Newspapers carried these stories, and those that wanted to, believed them.

Was Sam really gone? People wondered and hoped, until on a freezing day in March—four months after Sam Patch made his last jump—a farmer broke some ice to water his horses and found the answer no one wanted to hear.

Sam was caught in a game to break his record, and to go higher and higher. He had to play the game with a public that wanted too much. Poor Sam could not resist. He gave them the performance they wanted, but he also gave his life.

Then a strange thing happened. The people did not want to think of Sam as gone. Poems and stories about "Sam Patch, The Jumping Man" began to show up—in newspapers, in magazines, in books. They pictured a new, more exciting Sam jumping off heights he had never jumped and in places—like London and Paris—that Sam had never even been. Never mind what the farmer found in the frigid waters of the Genesee River—to the young America of the 1830's and 1840's Sam Patch lived.

Writing / Journal Activities

1. The Story

Write three important things that you learned from reading or listening to the story, "Sam Patch — The Man Who Jumped to Fame."

2. Find The Word

Copy the ONE WORD in each row that best describes Sam Patch.

Read Across →

1. stern, athletic, timid

2. brave, smart, sneaky

3. cowardly, bright, vigorous

4. entertaining, old, shy

3. Search And Find

Find the word (or words) closest to the meaning of the underlined word in each sentence. Then, copy the sentence, using the word (or words) in place of the underlined word.

1. The old farmer brought his two horses to a halt.
   stop   hesitation   slow down   gallop

2. The two horses clumped to a stop.
   thumped   clattered   staggered   wandered

3. The bridge spanned the river.
   went under   touched the edge of   went across   fell into

4. He looked down at the swirling waters.
   deep   turning   glistening   dirty

5. Both Sam Patch and the bear survived.
   lived   were injured   died   disappeared

6. The farmer was surprised by what he found in the frigid waters.
   swirling   still   lukewarm   cold

Let's Talk – Discussion Activities

4. Think It Through

Give as many answers as you can for each question.

—What do you think this means: "Something inside made him keep going."

—After Sam Patch died, some people believed that he was still alive. Do some people act the same way nowadays when someone famous dies? Try to explain why.

5. Take A Side

Here are two opinions on the same subject. Take one side or the other, and then give all the reasons you can for the side you take.

Should we admire someone who puts his life in danger to entertain us?

—"Sam Patch was great. We need more men and women like him."

—"Sam Patch was stupid for doing the things he did. The people who encouraged him were stupid too."

6. Then And Now

Compare the past with the present. Give as many answers as you can.

—People who take chances to entertain us the way Sam Patch did are called "daredevils." Name three or more hobbies or occupations that are likely to have daredevils today.

Cooperative Group Activities

7. Imagine

Make up an 1820's newspaper front page with a number of different stories describing some of Sam Patch's adventures.

8. Look Back

Select one of the events shown on the timeline for this story. Use other books or articles to gather more information about the event, and try to find out why the event was important. Present the information to the class.

1830

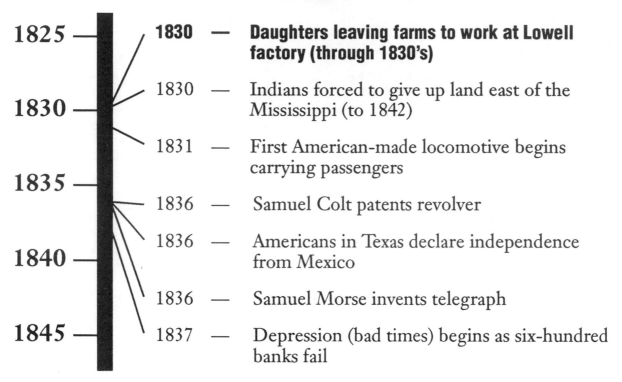

1830	—	**Daughters leaving farms to work at Lowell factory (through 1830's)**
1830	—	Indians forced to give up land east of the Mississippi (to 1842)
1831	—	First American-made locomotive begins carrying passengers
1836	—	Samuel Colt patents revolver
1836	—	Americans in Texas declare independence from Mexico
1836	—	Samuel Morse invents telegraph
1837	—	Depression (bad times) begins as six-hundred banks fail

What Else Was Happening?

Though most Americans still lived on farms or in small towns in the 1830's, more and more factories were being built. As factories started, and then grew, the towns and cities around them grew larger.

American inventors were discovering new ways of doing things, and other Americans seemed willing to invest money in their ideas. Workers, too, were willing to take on new tasks in a land rich in such natural resources as coal, wood, water power, and fertile soil.

During the 1830's new and better ways had to be found to haul raw materials and manufactured goods to and from these growing towns and cities. Water canals were dug to move people and products over long distances, and railroad lines were just beginning.

America was on its way to becoming an industrial nation.

#6

The Ladies of Lowell

The workers who lived through the collapse of the factory near Boston on that fateful day in January, 1860, would never forget the horror as long as they lived. One moment, shortly after five in the evening, hundreds of workers in the huge factory were tending the whirring machines that transformed cotton into cloth. The next moment, the men and women workers were startled by a shaking of the floors beneath them and a deafening rattle.

The floors were giving way!

As the five floors collapsed—each a hundred yards long—tons of machinery crashed down. The workers on each floor screamed out their terror as they tumbled crazily in all directions. Men and women were caught in a nightmare of smashed machines, falling bricks, and twisted iron. Some miraculously scratched and crawled their way to safety, but many others lay buried under tons of debris.

What a terrible end of the dream of Francis Lowell...

Almost fifty years before, in 1812, Francis Cabot Lowell was visiting a factory in London that manufactured cloth. Lowell was a successful Massachusetts businessman. He was in England for a rest, and while there he decided to visit some factories. At that time, raw cotton would be spun into spools of thread at one factory, and then the spools would be shipped to a second factory to be woven into cloth.

As young Lowell watched the machines spinning out their endless rolls of thread at one factory and bolts of cloth at another, a tremendous idea struck him. He did not, however, share his thoughts with anyone in England. Instead, he visited more factories, studying the machinery carefully, and—always—asking questions.

On the trip back to the United States, Lowell, mulled over what he had seen and heard in England. When he arrived back in New England, Lowell sought out a bright mechanic he knew named Paul Moody. Moody agreed to help him. Lowell's idea, or dream, began—a dream to build a new kind of factory that would spin cotton into thread and thread into cloth all under one roof. It had never been done before.

Next Lowell found men willing to invest their money in his idea. And, finally, he found a place not far from Boston alongside a fast moving stream that would provide enough power.

One question remained. *Who would work in the factory?* America was still a country of farms and farmers, not factories and factory workers. In England Lowell had seen wretched looking men and women beaten down from years of dismal factory work. It was not a pleasant sight, and he wanted no part of this wretchedness brought to New England.

The workers would be part of the dream too.

Courtesy, Museum of American Textile Industry

Each daughter would work a year or two and then return to the farm with a tidy sum of money.

Lowell would not hire workers to stay on year after year until they were beaten and exhausted. Instead, he would hire the daughters of New England farmers. Each daughter would work a year or two—possibly three—and then return to the farm with a tidy sum and a feeling of independence that the money gave her. It does not sound like much today—a chance to bring some money into a marriage, or a chance at independence for working a 12 to 14 hour day—but it would be very attractive to the young ladies of that day. What's more, the factory would build nice looking houses where a few older women could supervise the young ladies when they were not working.

When Lowell's first factory was completed, the young farm girls came from all over New England. They stayed a year or two and returned to the farm with money saved. Meantime, the factories produced large amounts of cloth at handsome profits. In the 1820's and 1830's more factories following Lowell's dream were built around Boston. The towns around each factory grew larger and larger. Lowell's dream was working. Visitors came from all over the world to watch and admire how well the young ladies worked.

But even a dream must come to an end. By the 1840's changes began to creep into the system. The demand for cloth was so great, that men and women immigrants from Europe were hired. Instead of living in nicely kept dormitories, they were housed in overcrowded "shanty towns." Instead of working a year or two, they stayed on year after year. The dream was beginning to shatter.

When the factory building crumbled to the ground that January evening in 1860, it signaled the end of Lowell's dream. When the iron pillars stopped their twisting, and the last of the machinery and bricks had thundered to the ground, the cries of the trapped workers could be heard. Rescuers scurried through the darkness to lift aside the debris and free the injured. The rescue efforts went slowly, and then some four hours after the collapse one of the rescuers accidentally dropped a lighted candle. The candle's flame licked at an oil soaked bundle of cloth. Flames raced through the debris stopping any further rescue efforts. The next morning the survivors could count ninety dead. The charred remains of the fallen factory stood as a silent reminder of a dream faded and then ended by years of change.

Writing / Journal Activities

1. The Story

Write three important things that you learned from reading or listening to the story, "The Ladies of Lowell."

2. Find The Word

Copy the ONE WORD in each row that best describes Francis Cabot Lowell.

Read Across →

1. careless, clever, selfish

2. silly, shy, bright

3. thoughtful, entertaining, jolly

4. lazy, ambitious, slow

3. Search And Find

Find the word (or words) closest to the meaning of the <u>underlined</u> word in each sentence. Then copy the sentence, using the word (or words) in place of the underlined word.

1. The workers would never forget the <u>collapse</u> of the building.
   twisting   burning   destruction   falling down

2. Lowell <u>mulled over</u> what he saw.
   grew angry   remembered   laughed about   thought about

3. Lowell found men willing to <u>invest in</u> his idea.
   put money into   tell about   recommend   steal

4. He had seen <u>wretched</u> looking men and women beaten down from years of factory work.
   foreign   miserable   strange   ignorant

5. The machines <u>transformed</u> cotton into cloth.
   weaved   changed   spun   molded

6. <u>Immigrants</u> were hired to work in the factories.
   strangers   people from another country   poor workers   people from farms

Let's Talk – Discussion Activities

4. Think It Through

Give as many answers as you can for each question.

—Why do you think so many farmers allowed their daughters to work at the factories in Lowell?

—Do you believe that Francis Cabot Lowell made America a better or a worse country? Explain.

5. Take A Side

Here are two opinions on the same subject. Take one side or the other, and then give all the reasons you can for the side you take.

Was it a good idea to let young women work in factories?

—"Letting young women work in factories was a poor idea."

—"Lowell's idea of having young women work in factories made a lot of sense."

6. Then And Now

Compare the past with the present. Give as many answers as you can.

—In what ways is it good for a worker to work in a large factory today? In what ways is it bad?

Cooperative Group Activities

7. Imagine

Make up two newspaper advertisements that encourage young women to come to work in the factories for Lowell.

8. A Look Back

Select one of the events shown on the timeline for this story. Use other books or articles to gather more information about the event, and try to find out why the event was important. Present the information to the class.

1847

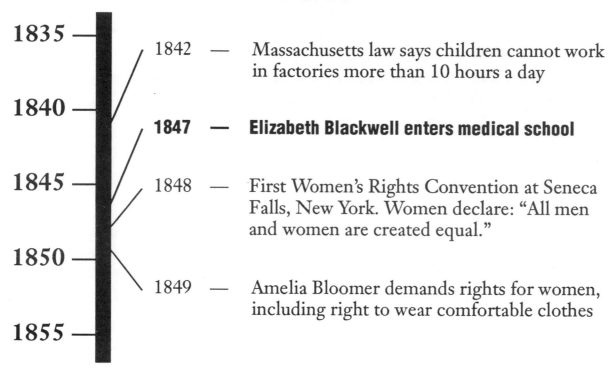

1835

1842 — Massachusetts law says children cannot work in factories more than 10 hours a day

1840

1847 — Elizabeth Blackwell enters medical school

1845

1848 — First Women's Rights Convention at Seneca Falls, New York. Women declare: "All men and women are created equal."

1850

1849 — Amelia Bloomer demands rights for women, including right to wear comfortable clothes

1855

What Else Was Happening?

Early American women had many duties, but few rights. A woman's husband was her master, and all of a family's money and property belonged to him. If a husband and wife separated, everything—including the children—belonged to the husband. People believed that women were weaker and not as bright as men. Education, they felt, was for men only.

By the 1840's, some women began pointing out that these ideas were wrong and that women deserved more rights. In the West the family depended on the wife and mother for survival. In the North women proved to be capable factory workers, and when a husband died, the widow who took over his business often did as well as the man.

#7

The Stubborn School Teacher

The professors at the medical school were shocked. Who ever heard of a woman doctor? And, yet, here was this Cincinnati school teacher—a woman!—sending an application to attend the Geneva Medical School of Western New York. *How ridiculous! A doctor had to be smart,* the professors told each other. *A doctor had to be able to stand the sight of wounds, and blood, and sick people.*

A woman was not smart, and she would probably faint at the first sight of anything unpleasant. A woman belonged at home, taking care of children, or teaching, or working on farms, or doing the special kind of work set aside for them in factories. But a woman doctor? How ridiculous.

The professors agreed—it was not a good idea for a woman to attend the Geneva Medical school. This was 1847. No medical school in the country had ever accepted a woman student. However, there was one problem. An important doctor had written a letter to the school recommending this stubborn school teacher. The professors did not want to offend the doctor, and so they decided to pass the application on to the medical students at the school and let them decide. If the students voted to let her in, she would be accepted. This sounded safe enough to the professors. After all, surely the students knew that a medical school was no place for a woman.

The professors were not prepared for what happened next. Of course, the students knew that medical school was no place for a woman. *The idea was silly!* But when it came time to vote on whether or not to accept her, one of the students announced that he had an idea. Why not, just as a joke, vote this woman—what was her name? Elizabeth Blackwell—into the college. The other students agreed that it would be a great joke to play on the professors. And so, Miss Blackwell's application was approved.

The students thought this was a big joke, but that was because they did not know Elizabeth Blackwell.

Elizabeth was born in Bristol, England, in 1821. She came to America with her family when she was 12. She was one of nine children, and when her father died when Elizabeth was still a teenager, the family struggled to make a living. Elizabeth became a school teacher. It was as a school teacher that she became interested in medicine. She read every book on medicine that she could find, and when a medical school professor took an interest in her and lent her some medical books, she read them all.

Elizabeth decided to become a doctor. *Never mind that women just did not become doctors.* She sent applications to one medical school after another, but the answers were always the same. No American medical school had ever accepted a woman. Elizabeth Blackwell, however, was too determined—or stubborn—to just give up. Then a letter came from the Geneva School of Medicine of Western New York, and Elizabeth was off to medical school.

Elizabeth soon discovered that the male students at the school resented her. They played tricks and made fun of her. They reminded her every time they could that her being there was a mistake, and that she really did not belong. When she visited the town near the school, the townspeople were no better. They ignored or made fun of her, too.

Everyone, even the professors, thought of her as some sort of a joke. Elizabeth however, did not think the matter funny at all. Nothing, no one, discouraged here. She stuck to the same stubborn determination that got her there in the first place. She studied as hard as she could. She asked the right questions, and she always seemed prepared in class. Two years later, Elizabeth had an answer for all the unkind remarks. Dr. Elizabeth Blackwell, the first woman doctor in American history, graduated as a top student.

"Dr. Blackwell," however, was in for more disappointments. When Elizabeth went to practice medicine, she heard the same comments again and again from patients: "What do you mean you are a doctor? You're not a man. I want a man doctor."

The talk bothered her, but it did not stop her. She left for Europe to study in the best medical schools in the world—in London, in

Courtesy, Smithsonian Institution

Elizabeth Blackwell had led the way

Paris, in Berlin. When she returned to the United States, she knew more about medicine than most American doctors. Unfortunately, things were not better. To patients Elizabeth Blackwell was still "that woman doctor."

Well, Dr. Blackwell thought, there had to be an answer. At this time, no doctor wanted to set up a practice in the poor neighborhoods of New York's east side. Dr. Blackwell decided to start a clinic right in the middle of the poverty of this east side. The people of these slums now had a choice: They could go without a doctor, or they could go see the "woman doctor." At first, the patients complained, but Elizabeth Blackwell soon won them over.

Elizabeth did not stop there. America's first woman doctor started New York's first clinic for woman and children. When the Civil War broke out in 1861, forty year old Dr. Blackwell battled with politicians in Washington until she finally convinced them to let her train women as nurses to take care of the war's sick and wounded. In 1868, Elizabeth opened the first medical school for women, and for the next thirty years, both in America and England, Dr. Blackwell trained women to be doctors. Being a doctor was still not easy for the women who came after her. There were jokes, and sly comments. But other women doctors could always look to Elizabeth and know that it must have been even more difficult for her.

Elizabeth Blackwell died in 1910 in Hastings, England at the age of 89. There were a number of women doctors in America at that time, and, everyone agreed, Elizabeth Blackwell had led the way. Dr. Blackwell's medical career began as a joke played by a group of medical students. When it ended, Elizabeth Blackwell—America's first woman doctor—had the last laugh.

Writing / Journal Activities

1. The Story

Write three important things that you learned from reading or listening to the story, "The Stubborn School Teacher."

2. Find The Word

Copy the ONE WORD in each row that best describes Elizabeth Blackwell.

Read Across →

1. ambitious, wealthy, frightened

2. tricky, persistent, worrisome

3. dull, irresponsible, studious

4. shy, forgetful, tenacious

3. Search And Find

Find the word (or words) closest to the meaning of the underlined word in each sentence. Then, copy the sentence, using that word (or words) in place of the underlined word.

1. The professors did not wish to offend the doctor.
   weaken   fire   displease   commend

2. Elizabeth kept her determination while at medical school.
   dream   study habits   quiet way   strong desire

3. The other students resented Elizabeth.
   disliked   tricked   fooled   got along with

4. Elizabeth practiced medicine in a poverty neighborhood.
   old   central   middle class   poor

5. Elizabeth decided that she would initiate a new clinic.
   work in   plan   start   design

6. Elizabeth Blackwell had pioneered the way for other women.
   chosen   shown   led   selected

Let's Talk – Discussion Activities

4. Think It Through

Give as many answers as you can for each question.

—Why do you think the other students made fun of, and picked on, Elizabeth Blackwell?

—In what way did Elizabeth Blackwell make America a better place to live?

5. Take A Side

Here are two opinions on the same subject. Take one side or the other and then give all the reasons you can for the side you take.

Should certain jobs and occupations be for men only?

—"Yes. Women should be kept out of certain jobs and occupations."

—"A capable woman should be allowed to take on any job or occupation."

6. Then and Now

Compare the past with the present. Give as many answers as you can.

—Name five occupations that have few (or no) women in them today. Try to explain why.

Cooperative Group Activities

7. Imagine

Imagine that you could go back to the time Elizabeth Blackwell began medical school. Prepare and present a television program in which you interview different women. The women tell you what jobs they are allowed to have, and what jobs are closed to them.

8. A Look Back

Select one of the events shown on the timeline for this story. Use other books or articles to gather more information about the event, and try to find out why it was important. Present the information to the class.

1849

1835

1840

1845

1850

1855

1843 — Many pioneers moving to Oregon

1846 — War with Mexico begins

1847 — Mormons settle Utah

1848 — Treaty ends war with Mexico—U.S. gains land in Southwest

1849 — California Gold Rush is on

What Else Was Happening?

The Mexican government encouraged Americans to settle on the Texas territory during the 1820's. At that time Texas was still a part of Mexico. In 1835 the Americans who had settled in Texas revolted against the Mexican government and asked the United States to "annex" or take over Texas. When the U.S. refused, the Texans declared that Texas was an independent country.

Some ten years later, in 1845, the United States did finally allow Texas to come into the Union as the 28th state. Mexico was very upset with the U.S. for taking over Texas. As far as Mexico was concerned, Texas was still a part of Mexico. When the U.S. sent troops into Texas, a war broke out that lasted from 1846 to 1848. At the end of the war, Mexico was forced to give up the huge territory, including California, that now makes up America's Southwest.

#8

The Gold Rush Days

Half buried in the desert, the bleached bones of mules and oxen stood out as warning signs to the pioneers who passed. Along with the clothing and furniture scattered about the trail, the bones reminded the men and women rolling by in their covered wagons that others had tried to cross the desert—and failed. The pioneers who passed such scenes may have had moments of doubts, but they always pushed on. Ahead lay California—and gold!

The spark that drove these men and women west was touched off on a January day in 1848. Men working to build a sawmill for John Sutter just outside of Sacramento, California, discovered specks of gold on his land. When they told Sutter of their find, Sutter swore them to secrecy. After all, he reasoned, who wanted thousands of gold seeking strangers trampling over the 50,000 acres of land he owned. Sutter soon discovered, however, that holding back such news was like trying to stop a rampaging river in early spring.

Over the next few months the news spread up and down California. Then people living in the East began hearing "wild" stories about gold being discovered in California. Most of the Easterners passed these stories off as "crazy rumors"—until December 5, 1848. On that day, James J. Polk, the President of the United States, announced that gold had, indeed, been discovered in California.

The gold rush was on!

Thousands of people living in the East now sold or gave away their belongings. They bought or traded for every kind of gold mining equipment they could get their hands on—most of it useless. Then they had to decide on a route to get to California. They soon discovered that there was no "easy" way.

Gold-seekers who took covered wagons across the overland route found plenty of danger. What do they do when the wagons break down? When they run out of water? When they go through country that has no grass the animals can feed off of? How do they get over the mountains when they reach Utah and Nevada? How do they cross a desert that has to be crossed in 24 hours in order to survive? And, how do they get over the Sierra Nevada Mountains before the snow falls?

Little wonder then, that some pioneers looked to the sea for what they thought would be an easier, safer route. Every kind of sailing ship was put into operation. Any old, abandoned ship—its bottom rotted, its mast splintered—was hauled off mud banks to sail again. Never mind that she had been put aside as unseaworthy! A little patch work here, some fixing up there, a few extra berths added, and the owner claimed that she would be ready to sail. It was bad enough that every broken down and worn out ship was being readied for California, but captains with little or no experience in sailing dangerous waters were pressed into service to sail them.

There were two sea routes to California. One stopped at the Isthmus of Panama, and the other went around the tip of South America. The companies that sold tickets for the sea route to the Isthmus of Panama promised a quick Atlantic sailing, followed by a simple 75 mile hike across the isthmus, and finally, an easy northward sail to California. A look at the map made the story sound convincing. Travel time? *Oh, six weeks, maybe seven*, the company claimed. Not bad at all, thought the gold-seeker who had never been to sea in his life. He paid his two or three hundred dollars and boarded the sailing ship.

When the overcrowded ship finally landed in Panama—if it did not sink on the way—the passengers discovered conditions that the maps did not show. The Isthmus was a steaming jungle of thick undergrowth with disease carrying insects everywhere. The trails were torturous. The rivers were narrow and winding with dangerous rapids. For the travelers who survived these dangers—and many did not—the worst was yet to come!

While there seemed to be enough ships for the voyage south to the Isthmus of Panama, there were very few ships to take passengers from Panama to San Francisco. Once a ship reached San Francisco, many members of the crew were bitten by the gold bug too. They abandoned ship and joined the passengers in the dash for the California gold fields. And so, because there were not enough crewmen, hundreds of ships lay abandoned and at anchor in San Francisco Bay.

Meanwhile, back at Panama, mobs waited in the miserable heat. When a ship finally arrived, people surged aboard and crammed every bit of space. Once the ship set sail, the hardships were far from over. A ship heading north to California often ran into prevailing winds that drove it further and further west. Some ships were blown most of the way to Hawaii before they could catch a favorable wind. The exhausted gold seekers who finally reached California by ship had often been gone some five months—as long as those who had taken the so called longer overland routes.

There was another route to California. For centuries ships had sailed from the Atlantic into the Pacific by going around Cape Horn at the southern tip of South America. This was still the only way to send large supplies to California, and the cargo ships that took this route took on passengers. The voyage "around the Horn," as it was called, was one of the most treacherous in the world. Winds forced sailing ships far south of their route into the freezing Antarctic. Gales smashed ships against uncharted reefs and rocks. A ship taking this route could save time by cutting through the Strait of Magellan, but only the most experienced sea captain would dare. Ships with rotted bottoms and inexperienced captains were hardly a match for the cross currents, riptides, massive storms, towering cliffs, and uncharted rocks. Many passengers who made the trip "around the Horn" later described their horror at seeing the floating wrecks of other ships.

There was, however, one bright light to these sad stories. The voyage around the tip of South America proved how good American built clipper ships could be. With more and more people going to California, there was a need to get more supplies and equipment there as soon as possible. Speed meant money. And the fastest sailing vessels in 1849 were the clippers. Clippers were thinner, sleeker, sailing ships with clean lines, and long, sharp bows. Strongly built, and rigged to get their fastest speed in hard winds, the clippers could

Courtesy, California State Library

The ship companies promised a quick, safe sailing.

outdistance any sailing vessel afloat. The average sailing ship made the voyage in six or eight months. The sleek clipper averaged a little more than four, and if the winds were right, could make it in three. These ships did not carry a large cargo, but getting the cargo there fast was more important.

Only a few of the people who came to California in search of gold, "struck it rich." California's real treasure, however, was not gold. Its real treasure turned out to be the brave men and women who came in search of gold, but stayed on and made California into a great state.

Writing / Journal Activities

1. The Story

Make up three good questions about the story, "The Gold Rush Days." Write the answer after each question.

2. Find The Headline

Here are three newspaper headlines. Copy the ONE headline that tells the main idea of the story the best.

1. Gold Seekers Sail to San Francisco Harbor

2. Gold Seekers Face Many Hardships on Way to California

3. Gold Seekers Strike It Rich in California

3. Take It Or Leave It?

Here are some things you might have wanted to take in your covered wagon if you were on your way to California in search of gold. If you only had room for THREE items, which would be the best three things to take to help you survive the journey safely. Write down your answers.

U.S. flag	grease for the wheels	map of Panama
book to read	books on gold mining	box of tools
table	big dog	compass

4. Did He Say That?

Here are six statements. Copy the THREE statements that might have been made by someone looking for gold in California.

1. "I came to California after I heard what President Polk said."

2. "I took the overland route in a covered wagon. It didn't take long at all."

3. "We really suffered crossing that Isthmus of Panama."

4. "Yes, our voyage around the Horn was really enjoyable."

5. "I sailed on one of those slow clipper ships."

6. "Very few people here have struck it rich."

Let's Talk – Discussion activities

5. Think It Through

Give as many answers as you can for each question.

—What kind of person was likely to move to California in search of gold? What kind of person was likely to stay where he was?

—Why is gold still so valuable?

6. Take A Side

Here are two opinions on the same subject. Take one side or the other, and then give all the reasons you can for the side you take.

Is it a good idea to take a chance in order to get rich?

"We should admire people who are willing to take chances to get rich."

—"People who take chances on 'striking it rich' are foolish. Very few ever succeed."

Cooperative Group Activities

7. Imagine

Imagine that you are a gold seeker getting ready to leave for California in a covered wagon. You want to take items that will help you get there safely. Would you take—

1. a puppy or a large dog?
2. a book on mining or a compass?
3. a frying pan or five dozen eggs?
4. a map of routes to California or a map of California.
5. some reading books or some chairs with a table?
6. a large hat or needles and threads.

Explain each decision.

8. A Look Back

Select one of the events shown on the timeline for this story. Use other books or articles to gather more information about the event, and try to find out why the event was important. Present the information to the class.

1854

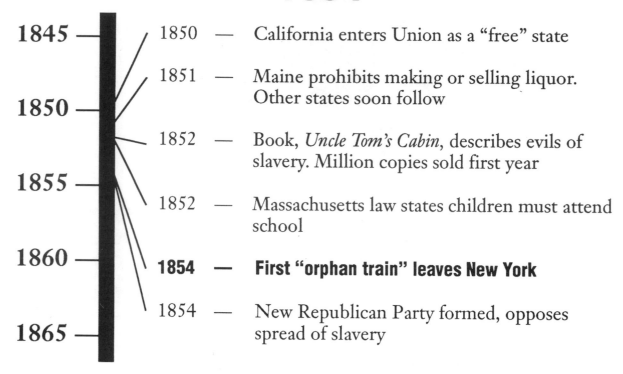

1845 —

1850 —

1855 —

1860 —

1865 —

1850 — California enters Union as a "free" state

1851 — Maine prohibits making or selling liquor. Other states soon follow

1852 — Book, *Uncle Tom's Cabin*, describes evils of slavery. Million copies sold first year

1852 — Massachusetts law states children must attend school

1854 — First "orphan train" leaves New York

1854 — New Republican Party formed, opposes spread of slavery

What Else Was Happening?

By the 1850's many Americans wanted to do something about America's problems. Because so many children were working in factories or wandering about the streets of large cities, some states passed laws that said children had to go to school. Other states made it against the law to sell liquor. Americans were also concerned with passing laws to help the poor, to help prisoners in jail, and to give more rights to women.

People who want to make changes to solve problems are called "reformers." During the 1850's many reformers believed that slavery was wrong. They called slavery "evil," and wanted laws passed that would do away with, or abolish, slavery all over the U.S. As the arguments over slavery began to boil over, there did not seem to be a way of solving America's most serious problem.

#9

The Orphan Train

By 1854 the sight of a train clicking across the Michigan countryside was not that unusual. The townspeople of Dowagiac and neighboring farmers had grown used to the locomotive roaring through their farmlands and pausing long enough to unload a shipment of goods before moving on. But this frosty morning was different. The train was coming to unload the strangest cargo any train had ever hauled to the small town. The cargo was not the usual farm tools or furniture, not woolen sweaters or heavy boots, but a shipment of forty-seven orphan boys.

On board the train the orphans pressed their cleanly scrubbed faces against the windows and stared out at a strange, new world. They were from New York City, and they had never seen a countryside before. First one boy and then another would shout out in surprise at what he saw—a herd of cows, a field of corn, a hayfield. Whenever someone shouted out a fresh discovery, the other boys would scurry from one side of the train to the other.

The idea of moving orphans out of New York City and into farm country belonged to a twenty-six year old minister from Connecticut named Charles Brace. Hoping to do all that he could to help poor people, he settled in New York City. New York was a bustling city of a half million people in the 1850's. The young minister noticed how each New Yorker seemed caught up in just trying to earn enough money to make a living.

Brace noticed something else. Somehow, lost in the bustle of activity were thousands of boys and girls—"children of the streets" he called them. Homeless, toddlers to teenagers, the children wandered about the city meant for grown-ups. Barefoot, usually in rags, soaked in the dust and grime of the city, the children foraged for food by day and slept in rubbish filled alleys by night. These orphans of the street begged, stole or formed gangs to prey on innocent citizens. Some of them peddled newspapers, apples, rags—anything to earn a few pennies.

Brace discovered that the children had no parents, or had been deserted. A report by the New York Chief of Police in 1852, reported that many of these children were forced to steal or rob in order to have enough food to eat. A few years before, Brace had visited some prisons in Europe. He felt certain that the young boys and girls he saw wandering the streets would become wretched prisoners like the ones he had seen, or they would go insane, unless—unless what?

America already had a number of what were called "orphan asylums." The people who ran these homes for children without parents made a point of telling everyone that they taught boys and girls right from wrong. Brace however, did not believe in orphan asylums. He argued: with so many children at an asylum, how could the few grown-ups there

Courtesy, Museum of the City of New York

Lost in the bustle of activity were the children of the streets.

give each boy and girl the amount of care, love, and affection each one needed?

Brace knew the problem a man and wife faced in a big city like New York. The child meant an extra mouth to feed at a time the young couple barely had enough money to feed themselves. And so, adults sometimes simply let their children wander about on their own. On the other hand, a young boy or girl on a farm, Brace believed, meant an extra pair of hands to milk the cows, thresh the wheat, till the soil, or feed the pigs. A child on a farm worked and contributed to the family and felt good about it.

In 1853 Brace and some other men living in New York City started an organization called the "Children's Aid Society." The So-

ciety rounded up 46 young boys who had been living on the streets. At the same time the Society found some farmers who lived around Dowagiac, Michigan, who said that they were willing to take a child to live with them. Arrangements were then made for workers from the Society to travel to Michigan with the orphans.

It sounded like a good idea, but would it work? Brace had seen the train off, then sat back and waited. It was easy enough for people to say yes we'll take the children, but once the orphans arrived how many of them would change their minds? The answer came a week later.

The boys had traveled by boat and train, and picked up one more orphan on the way.

They had arrived at the town on an early Sunday morning, tired, sleepy-eyed but excited. The townspeople had greeted them warmly, and, what is more, all 47 boys had been placed in homes. When Brace got the news one thought went through his mind—*this is only the beginning.*

He was right. In the 35 years that Charles Brace headed the Society, "Orphan Trains"—for that is what the trains were called—carried 70,000 boys and girls from the slums of the cities to farms all over the United States. The pattern stayed the same. Townspeople would let the Society know that they were interested in receiving orphans, and then announcements would be posted telling people in the town when the orphan train was due to arrive.

Once a train came in, the boys and girls were brought to a large hall or church. There the sight of so many children without homes touched the hearts of the farmers and townspeople.

And what about Brace's belief that if the orphans were given good homes they would not become criminals? The Children's Aid Society kept records. Very few of the boys and girls ever grew up to become criminals. Instead, they grew up to be farmers, workers, teachers, engineers, lawyers, judges, and even state governors.

The orphan trains stopped running by the late 1800's, but Charles Brace's idea of helping others inspires Americans to this day.

Writing / Journal Activities

1. The Story

Make up three good questions about the story, "The Orphan Train." Write the answer after each question.

2. Find The Headline

Here are three newspaper headlines. Copy the ONE headline that tells the main idea of the story the best.

1. Farmers Find Way to Get More Farm Workers.

2. Cities Discover Way to Get Rid of Wandering Orphans.

3. Orphans from Cities Find a Better Life.

3. Take It Or Leave It?

Pick out the THREE things or conditions that an orphan would NOT find at his or her new home. Write down your answers.

hard working people	cows	smiling children
warm meals	hungry people	barns
tall buildings	slums	a train station

4. Did He Say That?

Here are six statements. Copy the THREE statements that an orphan might have written in a letter about his new home.

1. "Everyone is mean to me here."

2. "I don't mind working hard."

3. "I get up so early now."

4. "It is crowded here."

5. "Working makes me feel important."

6. "I'm not sure where I will sleep tonight."

9

Let's Talk – Discussion Activities

5. Think It Through

Give as many answers as you can for each question.

—Do you think that the parents living in New York were "bad people," and the farmers and townspeople were "good people." Explain your answer.

—Why was Charles Brace so confident that the children who went to live on farms would not become criminals.

6. Take A Side

Here are two opinions on the same subject. Take one side or the other, and then give all the reasons you can for the side you take.

Should we help homeless people?

—"We should do all that we can to help the homeless people in our cities."

—"Homeless people will be better off if we let them take care of themselves."

Cooperative Group Activities

7. Imagine

Imagine that Charles Brace comes back in a time-machine and tours your town or city. Prepare and present a program where a number of reporters interview him and ask him what suggestions he has for solving the problem of homeless people in your town or city.

8. Look Back

Select one of the events shown on the timeline for this story. Use other books or articles to gather more information about the event, and try to find out why the event was important. Present the information to the class.

1856

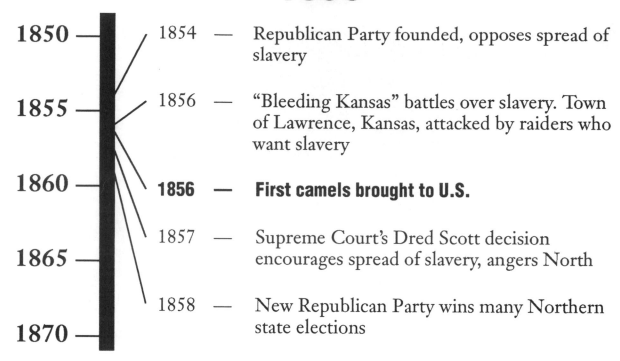

1850

1855

1860

1865

1870

1854 — Republican Party founded, opposes spread of slavery

1856 — "Bleeding Kansas" battles over slavery. Town of Lawrence, Kansas, attacked by raiders who want slavery

1856 — First camels brought to U.S.

1857 — Supreme Court's Dred Scott decision encourages spread of slavery, angers North

1858 — New Republican Party wins many Northern state elections

What Else Was Happening?

By the 1850's the Northern and Southern sections of the United States had grown very different from one another. The Northern section had many factories, more railroad lines, and many more people. On the other hand, the South's climate and soil had always been good for raising cotton on large farms called plantations. Southerners depended on slaves to work on the plantations.

As more and more Americans and immigrants settled on the lands in the West, a great debate, or argument, began. Northerners and Southerners knew that once a territory had enough settlers, the settlers would want it to become a state. While Northerners were anxious to keep the territories and new states free of slavery, Southerners wanted slavery to spread to the West. Southerners had one great fear: the politicians in the North and the West would work together to control the government in Washington, D.C. so that only laws would be passed that helped the industrial Northern states.

#10
Camels of the Old West

Early Americans never took the camel seriously. It was such an ugly animal with a strange bumpy back, eyes that popped out, and a stupid-looking face that was too small for its body. Then, something happened that made Americans take a second look at the "ugly" camel.

After the war with Mexico in 1848, the United States took over thousands of square miles of new territory. This territory stretched westward from what is now Colorado and New Mexico, through Utah, Arizona, and Nevada on to California. The new land was rich in minerals and fertile soil, but it had few trails and no railroads. How would Westerners, eager to work and settle on the new land, move supplies across the plains and deserts and over the mountains?

More than a century before, in the early 1700's, camels had been shipped to the Massachusetts colony on the east coast, but they were brought there only to be exhibited as a curiosity. No one dreamed of using such strange looking animals for transportation in America. We had horses and mules. After the war with Mexico, however, some Congressmen and Army officers thought that the camel would be perfect for carrying supplies in the new territory. After all, they argued, thousands of camels were used in parts of Asia and North Africa on terrain similar to the new territory. Why not ship some camels from Egypt to America and find out how well they would do here?

Seven years later, in 1855, Congress set aside the money for the purchase of camels. Two Army officers, Major Henry C. Wayne and Lieutenant David Porter, sailed to Europe and then to Egypt. In Egypt they purchased and shipped thirty-three camels back to the U.S. The camels arrived at a port near Galveston, Texas, and were then driven to Camp Verde, an army camp some sixty miles from San Antonio. It was here at Camp Verde that the great experiment would take place!

Army officers working with the camels soon made some interesting discoveries. The camel could not travel as fast as the horse, but when taught to kneel and rise, the animal could lift 600, 800, up to 1,000 pounds—much more than either a horse or a mule. The camel also proved perfect for desert travel. Drooping eyelids protected its eyes, and long eyelashes shielded it from the sun. When desert winds threatened to whip up the soil, the camel's nostrils closed tightly. A camel could drink as much as 30 gallons of water, and then travel for miles and miles through the fiercest desert heat without pausing for water. And, unlike the horse and mule, the camel could live off of the small, bitter-tasting bushes that dotted this arid land.

When more camels arrived at Camp Verde from Egypt some of them were sent on

By Laurel Long

The camel seemed perfect for the Southwest.

to Colorado and California. How would they do in the high country? The men who went over the mountains with the camels discovered that camels took the cold, the snow, the sleet, and the high altitude very well. The camel also proved as sure-footed over steep hilly slopes and high mountains as it had been on the prairie and the desert. And what is more, the camel surprised everyone by successfully swimming across mountain streams.

The faster horse might be best for short hauls, but this newcomer, with its uncanny ability to go long stretches without water, seemed ideal for the Southwest. By 1859, some government officials—sure that the settlers would be pleased—wanted to ship a thousand more camels to America. The Civil War interrupted the chance of bringing in more camels, however, and, perhaps, it was just as well. The camel might have been able to overcome treacherous deserts, and lofty mountains, but there were other obstacles in the way.

For one thing, the settlers were used to the beautiful well proportioned horse. Instead, here was an animal with a humpy back, a goose-like neck, and odd looking legs. Add to this, eyes that popped out, a split upper lip, a loosely hinged jaw, and a face that looked at once sad and stupid. One settler called the camel a "heap of ruins" and swore that the first time his horse saw a camel, the horse became so frightened that it tried to climb a tree. While the settler was probably exaggerating about the tree incident, horses, mules, and oxen did bolt at the sight of the oddly shaped "critter." To the settlers the camel was just plain ugly.

It is quite possible that the people who settled the Southwest night have, in time, accepted the camel despite its homely appearance. However, the camel's behavior exasperated even the hardiest of settlers. For example, if the camel felt mistreated—if someone overloaded him or whipped him—he would spit out a foul smelling saliva. Unfortunately, he was accurate up to ten feet. Other times, he chose to use a sneeze as a weapon—a sneeze that one settler described as "a mass of filth."

Of course, if the camel got really angry, he kicked or bit the nearest human, horse, mule, or ox. Even if a settler moved far enough away to escape the spit, sneeze, kick, bite, or smell, the camel could still annoy him. The "critter" had a long, piercing, cry that could rattle ear drums from quite a distance. As if all of this were not enough, the camel also had a terrible body odor and smelly breath.

And so, the settlers who had a warm fondness and love for their horses showed no such feelings towards this foul smelling animal they thought of as a "foreigner." Actually, camels were not "foreigners." Thousands of years before there was a United States, there were camels in North America. Some migrated northward across Alaska to Asia. Others moved southward to South America where their descendants, the llama and the alpaca, still live.

Still some American officials believed that the settlers could be won over in time. However, the Civil War that began in 1861 interrupted any more camel experiments. When the war finally ended in 1865, Americans were much more interested in using the railroad for hauling supplies than they were in either the horse or the camel. Some of the camels left over from the experiments were sent to zoos. Others died off in the open spaces. Time had run out. The camel would never find a place in America.

Writing / Journal Activities

1. The Story

Make up three questions about the story, "Camels of the Old West." Write the answer after each question.

2. Find The Headline

Here are three newspaper headlines. Copy the ONE headline that tells the main idea of the story the best.

1. Camels Fail to Find Place in U.S.

2. U.S. Uses Camels to Settle Western Lands.

3. Railroads Take Over Transportation in the West

3. Take It Or Leave It

Pick out the THREE words that a Westerner would have been most likely to use to describe his camel. Write down your answers.

sleek	loving	smelly
strange	friendly	cuddly
handsome	ugly	dependable

4. Did He Say That?

Here are six statements. Copy the THREE statements that might have been made by someone in charge of a camel.

1. "I can depend on him to behave."

2. "He can carry more weight than my horse."

3. "He stops for water all the time."

4. "I get mad when he spits that way."

5. "He's good at going over slopes and mountains."

6. "My neighbors think he is a lot of fun."

Let's Talk – Discussion Activities

5. Think It Through

Give as many answers as you can for each question.

—Is it right to like or not like a person because of the way the person looks? Explain your answer.

—Is it right to like or not like a person because of the way he or she behaves? Explain your answer.

6. Take A Side

Here are two opinions on the same subject. Take one side or the other, and then give all the reasons you can for the side you take.

Is it good to try out new ideas?

—"It's good to try new ideas and new ways of doing things."

—"Why try doing something new if the old way works fine?"

Cooperative Group Activities

7. Imagine

Imagine that you lived in the Southwest in the 1850's and that you were placed in charge of some camels. Write a letter to a friend telling him the many advantages of a camel. Predict the many wonderful uses that Americans will find for the camel.

8. A Look Back

Select one of the events shown on the timeline for this story. Use other books or articles to gather more information about the event, and try to find out why the event was important. Present the information to the class.

1859

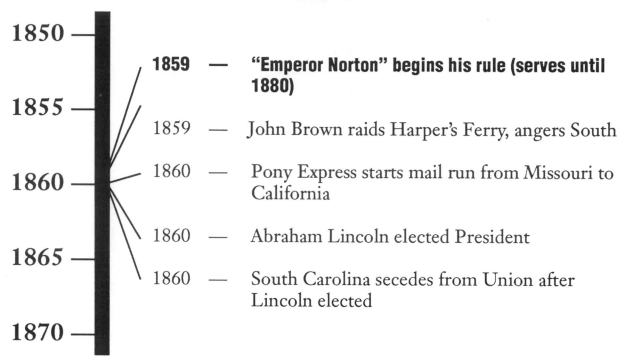

1850 ——

1855 ——

1860 ——

1865 ——

1870 ——

1859 — "Emperor Norton" begins his rule (serves until 1880)

1859 — John Brown raids Harper's Ferry, angers South

1860 — Pony Express starts mail run from Missouri to California

1860 — Abraham Lincoln elected President

1860 — South Carolina secedes from Union after Lincoln elected

---

What Else Was Happening?

In 1854 a group of Northerners started a new political party, called the Republican Party, to stop the spread of slavery. When Republican candidate Abraham Lincoln was elected President in 1860, Southerners were very upset. Lincoln had said that a nation could not survive "half free, and half slave." Southerners feared that Congressmen from the Northern and Western states would continue to outnumber them and would control the main government in Washington, D.C.

Soon after Lincoln's election, South Carolina announced that it was "seceding," or leaving, the Union. In time ten more states joined South Carolina to form the "Confederate States of America." Jefferson Davis, a Senator from Mississippi, was chosen to be the Confederate president.

President Lincoln declared that a state did not have the right to "secede," or leave the Union. He believed that it was his solemn duty to maintain the Union.

#11

Emperor Norton

You might expect this story to begin with "Once upon a time." After all, this is a story about America's first and only emperor, and everyone knows that America never had an emperor. Actually, however, America did have an emperor. His name was Joshua Abraham Norton the First, and he ruled from September of 1859 to January of 1880. At least he was Emperor as far as the people of San Francisco were concerned.

Emperor Norton ruled with some of the glitter, the pomp, and the ceremony usually reserved for the kings and queens of Europe. Thanks to the Emperor, people who walked the streets of San Francisco in the 1860's and 1870's were treated to a visual feast. His uniform was adorned with shiny brass buttons and golden strands. A long feather rose straight from his fancy officer's cap. And, as if this were not enough, passersby were dazzled by gold braided strands draped over each of his shoulders. The saber that hung from his side added a touch of regal splendor, while the gold topped cane he gripped tapped a signal that alerted citizens to the approach of His Royal Highness. He was indeed a splendid sight.

Pedestrians who viewed His Majesty on his walk bowed reverently, and the Emperor interrupted his brisk pace to return the compliment with a polite nod. When noontime approached, the Emperor looked about for an expensive restaurant worthy of the patronage of an Emperor of the United States and the Protector of Mexico. His entrance commanded the immediate attention of the owner or head waiter who seated him immediately, and served whatever suited the Emperor's fancy. The meal over, the Emperor might acknowledge that the meal was satisfactory, and begin to take his leave. The waiter would respond with a bow or a smile, but never, never with the presentation of a bill. After all, he was the Emperor.

Sometimes during one of his walks through the streets of San Francisco, the Emperor might enter a bank building where he would approach the nearest teller, present a check, and demand immediate payment. The teller would examine the ornate signature of Emperor Norton, stamp the back of the check, and then—though the Emperor had no account at any bank—proceed to hand the Emperor the sum noted on the check. The sum, however, never went beyond a check-writing limit the Emperor had imposed on himself. The limit? Twenty-five cents.

Sometimes the Emperor stopped at the Western Union telegraph office where he would announce to the telegraph operator that he had a few important messages he wanted delivered as soon as possible. The telegraph operator would exhibit the right amount of awe, and then reassure the Emperor that the messages he had written on scraps of paper would, indeed, be tapped out and delivered to the King of England, the Czar of Russia, or the Emperor of China.

Citizens of the Bay City made certain that the Emperor played a part in the life of San Francisco. He spoke at political rallies. He marched in parades. When dignitaries from around the would visited, the Emperor was properly introduced. Why, the state legislature even set aside a special chair for His Excellency. Nothing was too good for the Emperor.

Emperor Norton was not born an emperor—nor, for that matter, was he born in the United States. America's first Emperor was born in England and arrived in the U.S. in 1849 at the age of 30. He landed in San Francisco with quite a bit of money, and with the intention of making a lot more. Within a few years, thanks to some smart business dealings, Norton had a fortune of $250,000. You might think Norton would be satisfied with a fortune like that, but Norton was an ambitious man—eager to turn thousands into millions.

Norton had a scheme that he hoped would make him a millionaire. He would buy up all the rice in San Francisco! Once he had all the rice, he could charge people who wanted some almost any price. He would make a fortune! Norton began signing contracts to buy rice from everyone and anyone. He came close to "pulling it off," until something very unexpected happened. Three schooners sailed into San Francisco Harbor, their holds filled to the brim with—you guessed it—rice. Norton's scheme to "corner the rice market" sank like a torpedoed ship. The price of rice dropped dramatically, and Norton was left holding the bag. Instead of becoming a millionaire, he was

Emperor Norton was, indeed, a splendid sight.

penniless. In 1853, a poorer, but wiser Norton left San Francisco, and seemed to drop out of sight.

Five years later, a heavy-set man showed up in the office of the San Francisco Evening Bulletin. He handed the editor of the newspaper a piece of paper, and commanded the editor to print what was on the paper. The editor read the note, looked at the stranger in amazement, and then re-read the copy again: "I, Joshua Abraham Norton, declare myself Emperor of the United States and Protector of Mexico." The editor thought the proclamation amusing, and decided to print it. Citizens who read Norton's claim in the newspaper the next day also thought Norton's claim pretty funny. Over the next few weeks, Norton scribbled more proclamations that the editor decided to print. And then a strange thing began to take place. Instead of just laughing at Norton and the idea that he was an Emperor, the citizens began to "go along" with Norton's wild claims of sovereignty.

Over the years the people of San Francisco and the man who called himself Emperor built up a warm and wonderful understanding for each other. San Francisco protected and respected the "Emperor." Whenever they could, the citizens went along with his "royal requests." And, in his own way, the Emperor never took advantage of his exalted position. Invited to speak, he kept his speeches brief. Urged to attend a gathering, he took his leave before he could become a bore. Invited to eat without paying, he made certain not to eat too often at the same restaurant. Yes, he did cash worthless checks—but never for more than twenty-five cents.

For Joshua Abraham Norton, becoming an Emperor was a way of making life bearable again. For the people of San Francisco, having an Emperor was a delightful but harmless way of poking fun at things people take too seriously.

On a January afternoon in 1880, Emperor Norton was doing what he liked so much to do—promenading along a San Francisco street—when he unexpectedly sank to the sidewalk. Bystanders rushed to his aid, but it was too late. The Emperor was dead. The news saddened the people of San Francisco. They had grown fond of playing the "Emperor" game.

A few days later, a public funeral was held, and thousands came out to pay their last respects. After all, America had lost its first and only Emperor.

Writing / Journal Activities

1. The Story

Make up three good questions about the story, "Emperor Norton." Write the answers after each question.

2. Find The Headline

Here are three newspaper headlines. Copy the ONE headline that tells the main idea of the story the best?

1. Norton Loses Fortune When Rice Business Fails
2. Emperor Norton's Death Is Mourned by People of San Francisco
3. Citizens of San Francisco "Go Along" With Emperor Norton's Claims

3. Take It Or Leave It

Pick out the THREE words that citizens of San Francisco would have used to describe their feelings toward Emperor Norton. Write down your answers.

anger	warmth	hate
scorn	loathing	delight
revulsion	good humor	malice

4. Did A San Franciscan Say That?

Here are six statements. Copy the THREE statements that might have been made about Emperor Norton by a person living in San Francisco.

1. "I heard he just cashed another five dollar check at that bank."
2. "I understand he was once a successful businessman with a good deal of money."
3. "And I heard he really does have royal blood, and should be a king or emperor."
4. "Well, I will say that the people of San Francisco are really nice to him."
5. "I can't take his boring two hour speeches."
6. "He has given the people of San Francisco something to smile about."

Let's Talk – Discussion Activities

5. Think It Through

Give as many reasons as you can for each answer.

—In what way did it help Norton when he took on the role of "Emperor." In what way did it help the people of San Francisco?

—Are there magazines today that print outrageous stories about people who seem strange? Why do you think these stories are so popular?

6. Take A Side

Here are two opinions on the same subject. Take one side or the other, and then give all the reasons you can for the side you take.

Is it a good idea for people to "go along" with someone like Emperor Norton?

—"Having someone to laugh and joke about was a real help to everyone."

—"The people were foolish. Pretending he was an emperor kept people from thinking about important problems."

Cooperative Group Activities

7. Imagine

Make up a front page of a San Francisco newspaper that might have been printed during Emperor Norton's rule. Have stories in it about Emperor Norton. Include an editorial on whether or not we should try to get along with people who are different in some way.

8. A Look Back

Select one of the events shown on the timeline for this story. Use other books or articles to gather more information about the event, and try to find out why the event was important. Present the information to the class.

1862

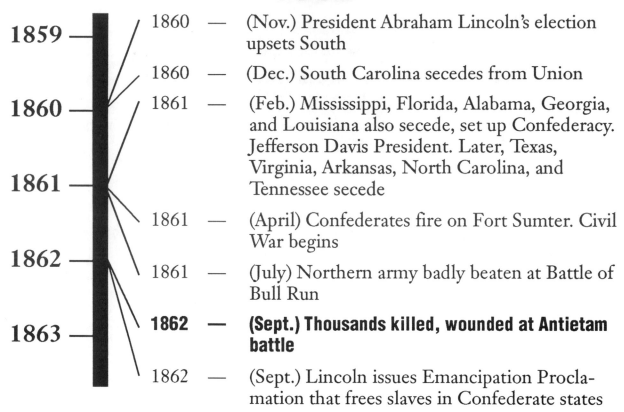

1859

1860

1861

1862

1863

1860 — (Nov.) President Abraham Lincoln's election upsets South

1860 — (Dec.) South Carolina secedes from Union

1861 — (Feb.) Mississippi, Florida, Alabama, Georgia, and Louisiana also secede, set up Confederacy. Jefferson Davis President. Later, Texas, Virginia, Arkansas, North Carolina, and Tennessee secede

1861 — (April) Confederates fire on Fort Sumter. Civil War begins

1861 — (July) Northern army badly beaten at Battle of Bull Run

1862 — (Sept.) Thousands killed, wounded at Antietam battle

1862 — (Sept.) Lincoln issues Emancipation Proclamation that frees slaves in Confederate states

What Else Was Happening?

Shortly after South Carolina seceded, Confederate forces shelled a group of Union soldiers stationed at Fort Sumter. The Civil War was on! The North claimed it was fighting to save the Union, while Southerners insisted that they wanted only to be left alone.

At first, neither side believed the war would last long. Each side thought that the other side would back away from more fighting. Then, as one terrible battle followed another, Northerners and Southerners came to realize that this war was not like any war they had ever fought before. By the 1860's factories could produce many more cannons and rifles, and railroads could haul huge amounts of equipment. Southerners and Northerners alike were shocked at the number of soldiers killed and wounded. Still, each side refused to give up.

#12

Bloody Antietam

Survivors of the battle called it "Bloody Antietam"—and with good reason. The clash of the Southern and Northern armies at Antietam Creek in Maryland on September 17, 1862, was the most frightful one day battle of the Civil War. The dead were everywhere—on open fields, by the creek, in the woods, on the bluffs. On one forty acre cornfield volleys of shot and shell had cut down every single cornstalk as if the stalks had been sliced by a giant knife. A survivor reported that he could have walked across the cornfield on the bodies of the dead. Another section of the battlefield was called "Bloody Lane." One body, doubled over a fence, had 57 bullets. *In but a single day of combat, over 23,000 Northern and Southern soldiers lay dead or wounded.*

Antietam marked the tragic end of a bold plan by General Robert E. Lee. Ever since the Southern states had seceded from the Union a year and a half before, Northern and Southern armies had hammered at one another—but always on Southern soil. Now, Lee planned to invade the North. He hoped to take his Southern army through Maryland and into Pennsylvania where he could destroy important bridges and railroads. Then, so his plan went, the war-weary North would capitulate. Lee was a brilliant and imaginative military leader, but not even he could have known that an amazing discovery would destroy his hope for an early end to the Civil War.

Lee's plan began twelve days before the Battle of Antietam. On the early morning of September 5, 1862, four lines of gaunt soldiers dressed in ragged, ill-fitting gray uniforms splashed into the cool waters of the Potomac River. Holding their muskets and shoes high to keep them from getting wet, the soldiers waded waist-deep to the Maryland shore half a mile away. For the next four days some 55,000 Confederate soldiers moved from the Virginia countryside onto the rolling green hills of Maryland in just this way.

Once in Maryland territory Lee had to capture a Northern stronghold that stood in the way at Harper's Ferry. Twelve thousand Northern soldiers were stationed there. Lee decided the best way to do this was to split his army into four groups, and so he called in one of his colonels and dictated "Special Orders 191" to him. These secret orders detailed how the army was to be split up.

One of Lee's generals argued with him not to split up the army. *It was too dangerous. The enemy could pounce on each group one at a time.* Lee knew this, but he had fought General George McClellan, the commander of the Northern army, before. He knew how slow and extra cautious he was. McClellan took a lot of time to make certain that everything was just right before he made any kind of move. Lee felt confident that by the time McClellan got around to fighting, Lee would have his four groups back as one army. Lee proceeded to order copies of "General Orders 191" sent to his nine commanding generals.

The news that Lee was on the move in Maryland hit the Northern capital of Washington D.C. like an artillery shell. President Abraham Lincoln ordered General McClellan to pursue and destroy the invading Southern army as quickly as possible. McClellan, with 90,000 men at his command, set out in search of the elusive Robert E. Lee. As the Northern army moved into Maryland, McClellan did not know exactly where Lee's army was headed.

Four days after leaving Washington, a company of weary Northern soldiers was ordered to make camp outside of Frederick, Maryland. Corporal Mitchell and Sergeant Bliss were among the soldiers who quickly unpacked and sought out places to rest. Most of the men were soon exchanging stories, smoking pipes, or brewing coffee. Mitchell and Bliss flopped to the ground and got ready for a few quick winks when Corporal Mitchell spied something on the trampled grass some five feet away. It looked like a piece of paper wrapped around something. This had been a campsite for the Confederate Army a few days earlier and the Southern soldiers had left a lot of litter behind. Bliss absently reached over, picked up the package and began unwrapping the paper.

Three fresh cigars came tumbling out. Mitchell broke into a broad grin, and handed one of the cigars to Sergeant Bliss. *What luck!* What a prize for two tired soldiers. While Bliss reached into his pocket for a light, Corporal Mitchell started to throw away the paper when something caught his eye. He took a closer look, and felt his body freeze. He let the cigar slip to the ground, and he showed the paper to Sergeant Bliss who blinked as he read it.

The corporal and the sergeant rushed the paper to Colonel Colgrave who immediately showed it to Colonel Pittman. Pittman lost no time in taking it to General McClellan's Northern Army headquarters. General McClellan was in a conference with some Frederick businessmen, but when he saw the look on Pittman's face, he allowed the colonel to interrupt the meeting and hand him the paper.

General McClellan let out a shout as he read the words, "Special Orders 191." Up to this point McClellan had been pursuing Lee blindly, uncertain of where he was and what he was going to do. *Here were the details of where Lee's army was and where it intended to go.* McClellan telegraphed a message to President Lincoln: "I have all the plans of the rebels, and will catch them in their own trap."

McClellan should have rushed his men to attack Lee's divided forces. Instead, he delayed another 16 hours. In the meantime, one of the businessmen who had been in McClellan's tent when the paper was delivered, made his way to the Southern lines. The businessman then told a Southern officer how he happened to be in McClellan's tent when someone brought him a piece of paper, and how overjoyed McClellan was. When Lee heard about this, he guessed that McClellan knew something about his plans. Lee would have to stop and make a stand. He chose Antietam Creek, near the town of Sharpsburg.

McClellan continued his sluggish march towards Lee. When he finally reached Antietam Creek and faced Lee, he let another day slip by. More troops were able to rejoin Lee. Finally, on September 17, four days after

Courtesy, The Bettman Archive

Survivors called it "Bloody Antietam"—and with good reason.

McClellan found out about Lee's battle plans, the two massive armies collided. The Northern soldiers, led by generals not as clever as the South's generals, charged again and again. The ragtag Southern army—exhausted from forced marches, many hungry and in rags, some without shoes—fought with stubborn determination. By nightfall, each side stood its ground.

The next day Lee took his shattered army back to Virginia. In one way, the battle was a victory for the North. McClellan had stopped the invasion of the North and forced the Southerners back to Virginia. But, in another way it was not. McClellan, with a much larger army and more equipment, had let a golden opportunity slip between his fingers. Armed with Lee's secret orders, he could have crushed the Southern army once and for all. Instead, he continued his slow and cautious ways, and the Southern army escaped to fight again.

Lee called the loss of the secret orders, "a great calamity." To this day, no one knows for certain how the orders were lost. The Civil War would grind on another two and a half years, but, because of the discovery of three cigars wrapped in a piece of paper, the South would never again be so close to victory.

Writing / Journal Activities

1. The Story

Make up three good questions about the story, "Bloody Antietam." Write the answers after each question.

2. Find The Headline

Here are three newspaper headlines. Copy the ONE headline that tells the main idea of the story the best?

1. McLellan Claims Victory at Antietam
2. Lee Moves North to End War But Returns to South After Battle at Antietam
3. Antietam Survivors Describe Terrible Loss of Lives

3. Take It Or Leave It

An artist drew these nine scenes to illustrate this story. Copy out the THREE scenes that do NOT belong.

three cigars wrapped in paper	General McClellan	a Northern farm
a Southern cotton plantation	a Northern warship	General Lee
tired Confederate soldiers	wounded soldiers	Antietam Creek

4. Did he Say That?

Here are six statements. Copy the THREE statements that might have been made by General Robert E. Lee.

1. "Let's fight on Northern soil for a change."
2. "I never like to take chances."
3. "My men are well rested and have the best uniforms."
4. "Both the North and the South lost many men at Antietam."
5. "I'm willing to do this because I know General McClellan is so cautious."
6. "I didn't mind losing those secret orders."

12

Let's Talk – Discussion Activities

5. Think It Through

Give as many answers as you can for each question.

—In what ways do you think that a civil war is worse than a war between two nations?

—Why do you think neither side was willing to stop the war even after the terrible battle of Antietam?

6. Take A Side

Here are two opinions on the same subject. Take one side or the other, and then give all the reasons you can for the side you take.

Is it better to be a cautious person or a person who is always taking chances?

—"It is better to be cautious."

—"It is better to be a person who is willing to take a chance."

Cooperative Group Activities

7. Imagine

Abraham Lincoln was one of our greatest presidents. Is it better to have a president who—

1. is a good speaker or who is well educated?
2. is intelligent or who has a great personality?
3. is charming or who is always calm?
4. is full of energy or who comes from a good family?
5. is creative or who knows how to pick the best people for a job?
6. has a great smile or who uses his time well?
7. cares about people or who is willing to take chances?

Answer using the same questions: Is it better to have a general who—

Be ready to explain your answers.

8. A Look Back

Select one of the events shown on the timeline for this story. Use other books or articles to gather more information about the event, and try to find out why the event was important. Present the information to the class.

1864

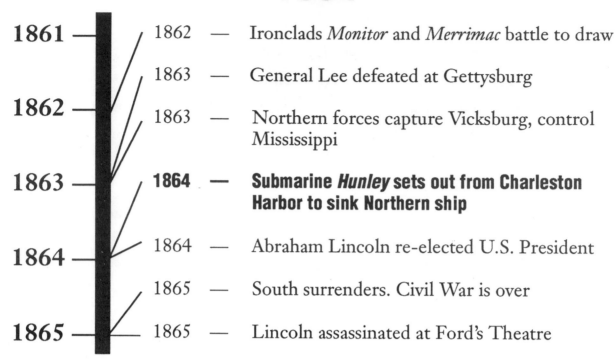

1861

1862

1863

1864

1865

1862 — Ironclads *Monitor* and *Merrimac* battle to draw

1863 — General Lee defeated at Gettysburg

1863 — Northern forces capture Vicksburg, control Mississippi

1864 — Submarine *Hunley* sets out from Charleston Harbor to sink Northern ship

1864 — Abraham Lincoln re-elected U.S. President

1865 — South surrenders. Civil War is over

1865 — Lincoln assassinated at Ford's Theatre

What Else Was Happening?

General Robert E. Lee commanded the Southern Army. He was a brilliant general. Though he had less men and less equipment, he won most of the early battles. Meantime, Northern ships blockaded Southern ports and kept needed supplies from reaching the South.

The Civil War dragged on for four years with heavy losses on both sides. When the Northern Army failed to defeat the South, many Northerners demanded that President Lincoln give up and allow the South to form its own nation. Lincoln, however, insisted that the North keep on fighting to save the Union.

When General Grant was placed in charge of the Northern Armies, the tide of battle changed. By 1865 the South had lost so many men and so much equipment it could no longer carry on the war. General Lee surrendered to Grant at Appomattox Court House in April, 1865.

#13

The Strange Mission of the Hunley

The seven men sat cramped closely to each other in a single line and strained to turn the metal crank that ran the length of the strange narrow craft. Their muscles ached with each turn and sweat trickled down their warm bodies. Breathing the thin foul air inside the narrow tube was turning out to be just as much work as turning the crank. Meantime, the light from the candles in the eery darkness turned each movement into weird shadows that flickered across the metal walls.

Ever since the 30 foot cigar-shaped craft had left Charleston Harbor, the hard work turning the crank had left little time to talk. Actually, there was very little reason to say anything; each man on board knew what the other was thinking. *Will we really be able to reach the target? Will we come out of this alive?* The men had good reason to wonder about their fate. They were on board the Civil War's version of a submarine—the *Hunley*, also known as the "Crew Killer."

By late 1862, a Northern sea blockade choked the Southern ports and kept products from flowing in or out. In its effort to find anything that might break the blockade, the Confederacy agreed to the construction of the *Hunley*. The *Hunley* was a primitive idea of what in later years would become the submarine. It was nothing more nor less than a reconstructed iron boiler, thirty feet long, four feet wide, and with a propeller shaft for cranking that ran along its length. Seven men inside turned a crank that rotated a propeller at the stern. In calm water it might make four miles an hour. Water tanks could be filled or emptied so that the submarine was able to submerge or rise to the surface. There was no periscope, no air pumps, no torpedoes, and no way for the men to move or stand. To see where it was going, the *Hunley* had to break the surface of the water just enough to open the hatch on top.

It was on such a crude craft that the crew of eight brave crewmen slipped out of the Charleston, South Carolina, harbor on a cool moonlit night in February of 1864. The original idea had been for the submarine to go to sea dragging a 100 yard line. When an enemy ship was spotted—so the idea went— the submarine would slip under the ship and keep right on going. Then a charge on the end of the line would smash against the enemy ship and send it to its doom. However, even the desperate Southerners soon realized the tactic of going underneath a warship was too risky. Instead, a pole with explosives on its tip was mounted on the Hunley. The idea was for the submarine to sneak towards the enemy ship and ram the pole into the unsuspecting enemy's hull.

But the story of the Hunley is not metal plates or explosive charges. The real story of the *Hunley* is the story of the volunteers on board the submarine as it inched towards a

By Laurel Long. From an early model courtesy, Smithsonian Institution

There it was! The *Hunley* closed in on its target.

1240 ton thirteen gun Northern warship on this moonlit November night. Each man on board had to be braver than any nation has the right to ask a soldier or sailor to ever be. The real story began months earlier when the first crew of volunteers sat inside the Hunley and prepared for a test run. A passing ship caused a small wave, or swell, and the swell spilled down into the open hatchway! The sub sank like a rock and all aboard were drowned.

Shaken by the experience, the Southerners raised the submarine, asked for—and got— eight more volunteers. Once again a swell of water sank the Hunley and claimed eight more lives. A shaken salvage crew raised the submarine from the ocean depths, and once again took on the awful task of removing the bodies of the crew. A third group of volunteers came forth. The third crew practiced a number of dives successfully. Everyone breathed easier.

A final test was scheduled, this time with people looking on to view the *Hunley's* ability to submerge and surface. The *Hunley* dove, and the onlookers waited—and waited. Hours past until the people on the shore finally had to accept their worst fears. The *Hunley's* third crew had suffered the fate of the other two.

Before volunteering, each crewman had been told in detail what had happened to the earlier crews. Now, General Beauregard, the commander of Confederate forces in this section of South Carolina, was having second thoughts about the venture. *Perhaps it was best to forget about the "Crew Killer" Hunley, and admit failure.* Three crews had been lost, the last crew included one of its inventors, Horace Hunley, for whom the submarine was named. Dared General Beauregard ask for volunteers a fourth time? Reluctantly, he agreed to one more trial. Another group of brave men came forth. This time the trial run went off well. But the real test was taking place now as the *Hunley* sought out its first Northern warship.

The officer on board the *Hunley* turned the valves that controlled the water tanks. The men on board felt the Hunley move upward until it broke the surface just enough for the officer to peer through the open hatch. The officer's eyes scanned the misty darkness. *There it was!* Off starboard lay the Northern warship, the *Housatonic.* The officer's hands turned the lever that worked two outside fins. He muttered a word of encouragement as the crew kept up a steady cranking motion. The *Hunley* closed in on its target.

On board the *Housatonic,* a Union sailor spotted the strange craft. He shouted an alarm, and the Northern warship moved towards the strange sight. Suddenly, the *Housatonic* was shaken by a giant explosion that blasted a huge hole in its stern. Water rushed in through the gapping hole, and black smoke billowed skyward. Within minutes, the crippled Union warship sank to the ocean floor, the first warship ever sunk by a submarine. The *Hunley* had been able to drift close enough to sink the enemy.

But was it really a victory? The force of the Housatonic's explosion had smashed against the tiny *Hunley*. The *Hunley* shuddered, tilted downward, then headed toward's the ocean bottom—its brave crew still on board.

Writing / Journal Activities

1. The Story

Make up three good questions about the story, "The Strange Mission of the *Hunley*." Write the answers after each question.

2. Find The Headline

Here are three newspaper headlines. Copy the ONE headline that tells the main idea of the story the best.

1. Brave Crews of *Hunley* Fail to Break Northern Sea Blockade
2. Surprise Southern Attack Sinks *Housatonic*
3. Northern Blockade Keeps Ships Out Of Southern Ports

3. Take It Or Leave It

Here are nine words that might be used in writing a story that describes the *Hunley* crews. Copy out the THREE words that do NOT belong here.

heroic	fainthearted	hardy
courageous	puny	daring
bold	audacious	delicate

4. Did he Say That?

Here are six statements. Copy the THREE statements most likely to have been made by a crew member on the *Hunley*.

1. "An officer made me join the crew of the *Hunley*."
2. "I'll be glad to get back to Charleston."
3. "This is a lucky ship."
4. "We want to break the Northern sea blockade."
5. "I'm tired."
6. "At least we have a safe ship."

Let's Talk – Discussion Activities

5. Think It Through

Give as many answers as you can for each question.

—Why are ships so important in time of war?

—In what ways are today's astronauts like members of the *Hunley* crew? In what ways are they different?

6. Take A Side

Take one side or the other. Give all the reasons you can for the side you take.

Does our government have the right to ask men and women to risk their lives on dangerous missions?

—"Yes, the government should be able to ask people to risk their lives in an emergency."

—"No, the government has no right to ask someone to risk his or her life for anything."

Cooperative Group Activities

7. Imagine

Prepare and present a program where a group of reporters interview a Southerner who has just volunteered to become a member of the fourth *Hunley* crew.

8. A Look Back

Select one of the events shown on the timeline for this story. Use other books or articles to gather more information about the event, and try to find out why the event was important. Present the information to the class.

1865

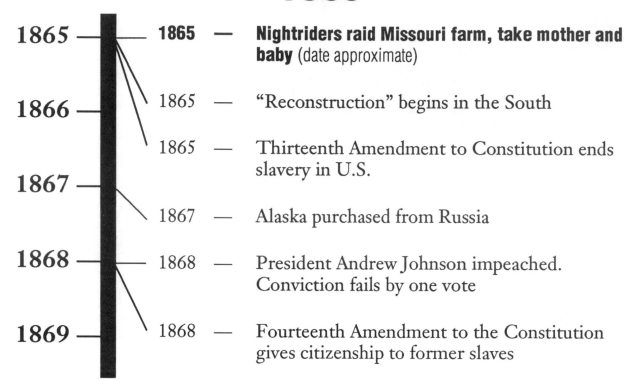

1865	Nightriders raid Missouri farm, take mother and baby (date approximate)
1865	"Reconstruction" begins in the South
1865	Thirteenth Amendment to Constitution ends slavery in U.S.
1867	Alaska purchased from Russia
1868	President Andrew Johnson impeached. Conviction fails by one vote
1868	Fourteenth Amendment to the Constitution gives citizenship to former slaves

What Else Was Happening?

Because most of the Civil War fighting had taken place on Southern soil, the South lay in ruins. Also in ruins and gone forever was a Southern way of life that depended on slaves working on plantations.

President Abraham Lincoln had planned to bring the Southern states back into the Union "with malice towards none, and with charity for all." Lincoln's sudden death kept this from happening. Instead, Northern Congressmen treated the Southern states as though they were a defeated nation. The Northern politicians did not want the Southern states to have any power in the government in Washington, D.C. African Americans were no longer slaves, but they still faced very difficult times.

#14

The Three Hundred Dollar Baby

At the first sound of the horses pounding their way up the dirt road, Moses darted out of his farmhouse and headed straight for the small cabin in back. "Nightriders," he muttered to himself, and—indeed—as the noise of the hoofbeats grew closer and closer, the old farmer knew he had little time to act if he wanted to save his nineteen year old slave girl, Mary, and her two children.

Moses Carver and his wife, Susan, had worked on their farm in the southwest corner of Missouri for some thirty years. The farm was not far from the Kansas border. Throughout the 1850's—and into the 1860's—armed bands of men had ridden back and forth across the Missouri-Kansas border, fighting and arguing with one another over whether Kansas should have slaves. Some of these men on both sides were so caught up in the fury of the slavery argument that they sometimes turned to home-burning, shooting, stabbings, and even hangings.

Some men—called Nightriders—had learned to take advantage of this confusion over slavery. Waiting until dark, they would swoop down on a farm and take off with whatever slaves they found. Instead of freeing the slaves, however, the Nightriders sold the kidnapped slaves for a handsome profit.

When Moses reached the cabin behind his farmhouse, he rushed in and grabbed Mary's four year old son. "Follow me," he yelled to Mary who sat holding her baby boy in her arms. Mary may have been too frightened to know what to do. She did not follow Moses. Moments later, the Nightriders burst into the cabin.

Back at the farmhouse Moses and his wife waited for quiet to signal that the Nightriders had left. When they could hear no more noise, the two of them rushed back to the cabin. A frightening silence greeted them—Mary and the baby she had held in her arms were gone! The Carvers were heartsick.

Moses Carver was a hard working white farmer. Six years before, when the work around the house and farm had become too difficult for his wife, he had purchased Mary. The Carvers had always treated her well.

The next day a man who knew his way around the Missouri and Kansas countryside agreed to go in search of the Nightriders. Moses promised the man some of his land and a racehorse if he returned Mary and her baby boy.

A few days later, Moses spotted the man galloping towards the Carver farm. Mary was nowhere in sight, but, as the man pulled up, Moses noticed a crumpled overcoat in his arms. There—nestled snugly in the folds of the coat—was Mary's baby boy! Moses quickly came to an agreement with the man: he would give him the horse for the return of the baby.

As the man rode off, Moses looked down at the child. Its black arms and legs were thin as sapling branches. The baby gasped, coughed, then gasped again. It was having trouble breathing. Moses shook his head sadly. This baby had the whooping cough. *Why had he given the man a racehorse worth $300 for this sickly child?*

Moses's wife, Susan, took care of the baby she called, "Carver's George." The infant's father had been killed in an accident before Mary was kidnapped, and it was not unusual to use a master's name in this way. "Carver's George" grew into a shy child with a high pitched voice. He remained thin and sickly-looking, and small for his age. Even so, there was something different, something very special about this little child.

"Carver's George" seemed so curious, so interested in things. He was always asking questions—especially about things that grew. *Why is this flower red? Why did this plant die? How does a tree grow from a seed? What makes it rain?* He collected everything—frogs, rocks, tree bark, feathers, grasshoppers, leaves.

As he grew older, young George had no books to read nor teachers to ask, but he did have a secret garden he had planted in the woods. Here he experimented to learn what made plants grow healthy. Neighbors called him "Doctor Plant," and often asked him how to make the plants in their gardens grow better. George realized that if he wanted to learn more about the world of nature he would have to go to school. However, even though the slaves were freed when the Civil War ended in 1865, the schools near the Carver farm were for white children only. If he wanted to go to school, he would have to leave home.

George was only ten years old when he said good-bye to the Carvers and started out on his own. For years, he wandered about Missouri and Kansas working as a farmhand, a laundry helper, or a cook. He scrubbed floors,

he baked bread, he washed clothes—he did anything to make ends meet. When not working, George went to school—the ones for black children. One day he changed his name from "Carver's George" to "George Washington Carver." At eighteen, he graduated from a high school in Minneapolis, Kansas.

George wanted to go to college, but very few colleges accepted black students in those days. When he finally found one that did, he was 25 years old. George was the second black student ever to attend Simpson College in Iowa. Two years later, he left to go to Iowa State Agriculture College. After he graduated from Iowa State College, he was placed in charge of the college greenhouse where he continued his experiments on plants.

Booker T. Washington had started the Tuskegee Institute in Alabama for black students. In 1896 he invited George Washington Carver to come to Tuskegee to run the agriculture department. Carver accepted—and it was here at Tuskegee that his real work began. For the next 47 years Carver devoted his life to showing farmers of the South—black and white—the best way to grow their crops.

Southern farmers had been planting cotton on the same land year in and year out for over a hundred years. Carver tried to explain to the farmers that planting cotton in this way wore out the soil. The cotton crops were getting worse each year. Carver urged the farmers to "rotate" their crops by planting peanuts some years instead of cotton. He explained how the roots of the peanut plant actually enriched the soil with minerals.

However, the farmers were so used to planting cotton, they refused to listen. Then, one year, the boll weevil pest destroyed so much of Alabama's cotton crop, the farmers had to plant something else. And so, they

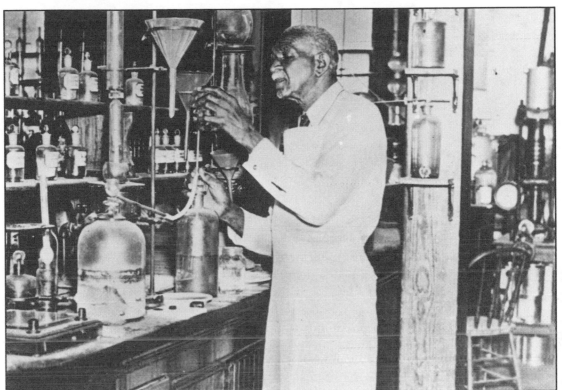

Carver was convinced he could turn the peanut into something useful.

planted peanuts. What happened, however, was not good either. The farmers had tons of peanuts that they could not sell.

Carver went back to his laboratory, convinced that he could turn the peanut into something useful. He crushed it, heated it, pounded it, mashed it, cooked it, boiled it, strained it, dried it. He knew which chemicals to add and which to take out, and changed the peanut into soap, cooking oil, face cream, coffee, wood filler, dyes, shampoo, metal polish, paper, ink, shaving cream, flour, milk, butter, and cheese. In all, he made over three hundred products from the peanut. *Now, there would be a market for peanuts.*

He did not stop there. He told the Southern farmer to plant sweet potatoes and soybeans too—and then found over 100 products that could be made from them. He also made boards from corn and sunflower, paint from clay, and soap from hog fat. His fame spread far and wide. Presidents and important people from all over the world visited his laboratory at Tuskegee. Large companies offered him huge salaries to work for them, but Carver always refused. He wanted to keep on helping farmers, showing them the best way to plant, to fertilize, and to conserve the soil.

Back in 1865, Moses Carver had wondered if the sickly baby he held in his arms was worth the three hundred dollar horse he gave. He had no way of knowing that one day this child would grow up to be a scientist whose work and ideas would be worth millions to farmers in the South and all over the world. George Washington Carver died in 1943. The tombstone placed at his grave reads, "He could have added fortune to fame, but... found happiness and honor in being helpful to the world."

Writing / Journal Activities

1. The Story

Make up three good questions about the story, "The Three Hundred Dollar Baby." Write the answers after each question.

2. Find The Headline

Here are three newspaper headlines. Copy the ONE headline that tells the main idea of the story the best.

1. Carver Becomes Famous and Wins Many Honors
2. Carver Uses Science to Help Farmers
3. Southern Farmers Learn to Plant Peanuts

3. Take It Or Leave It

Here are nine things that might have been seen on George Washington Carver's desk. Copy out the THREE items that do NOT belong here.

peanuts	letter from President	checkbook
soybeans	comic book	stock market report
test tubes	potato	science book

4. Did He Say That?

Here are six statements. Copy the THREE statements that George Washington Carver might have made.

1. "I like to study."
2. "I want to be famous."
3. "I ask a lot of questions."
4. "It's always better to grow cotton instead of peanuts."
5. "I enjoy helping other people."
6. "I want to make a lot of money."

Let's Talk – Discussion Activities

5. Think It Through

Give as many answers as you can for each question.

—What do you think someone might learn from studying about the life of George Washington Carver?

—Why do you think George Washington Carver refused to take a job that paid him more money?

6. Take A Side

Here are two opinions on the same subject. Take one side or the other, and then give all the reasons you can for the side you take.

What is the most important thing to consider when looking for a job?

—"Salary is the most important thing to consider in any job."

—"How much you enjoy the job—that is the most important thing to consider."

Cooperative Group Activities

7. Imagine

Imagine that George Washington Carver is alive today and writing a newspaper advice column. Make up such an "Advice from George" column with three (or more) questions sent in by readers, followed by Carver's answers. (Possible reader questions: "Should I drop out of school?", "Why should I go to college?", "What should I do when I feel like giving up?", "Why should I be curious?")

8. A Look Back

Select one of the events shown on the timeline for this story. Use other books or articles to gather more information about the event, and try to find out why the event was important. Present the information to the class.

1869

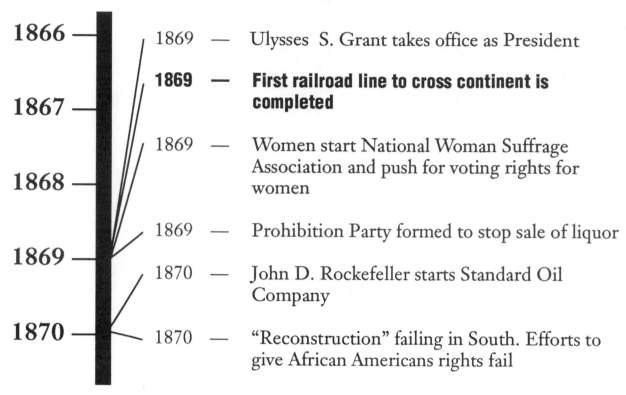

1866	1869 —	Ulysses S. Grant takes office as President
1867	**1869** —	**First railroad line to cross continent is completed**
1868	1869 —	Women start National Woman Suffrage Association and push for voting rights for women
1869	1869 —	Prohibition Party formed to stop sale of liquor
	1870 —	John D. Rockefeller starts Standard Oil Company
1870	1870 —	"Reconstruction" failing in South. Efforts to give African Americans rights fail

What Else Was Happening?

The construction of railroad lines all across the country made a great change in America. Manufacturers could now sell their products all over the country. As a result, huge corporations, sometimes called "Big Business," began to gain conrol of America's natural resources and manufacturing. John D. Rockefeller, for example, started a company that would take over the oil industry. "Big Business" built up many great industries in America, but it also created some serious problems.

Meantime, by 1870 efforts to give African Americans their rights were beginning to fail. Former slaves found life very difficult as they tried to find a place in American life and struggled to make a living.

#15

The Men Who Built the Railroad Across America

The husky man raised the silver hammer above his head, then slammed it down on the gold spike that had been placed beside the railroad track. Again and again he hammered at the spike and when, at last, the spike was driven all the way into the ground, the large crowd that had gathered around him this warm afternoon on May 10, 1869, broke into wild cheering. Two train engines that had sat motionless facing one another now inched forward until they almost touched each other.

The crowd had gathered at a place called Promontory, outside of Ogden, Utah. And now the telegraph operator at Promontory clicked out a one-word message for the crowds that had gathered in cities all over America: "Done!"

Yes, it was "done!" At long last, the dream of a transcontinental railroad — a railroad that stretched across America — had come true. Americans, with good reason, called the rail line "the greatest engineering feat of the century." There was a time, however, when the bosses of the Central Pacific railroad had cause to wonder if the dream would ever come true.

The building of the railroad line to connect the Atlantic with the Pacific had begun six years before — in early 1863. The Union Pacific started constructing a railroad line from Omaha, Nebraska, moving west. The Central Pacific started from Sacramento,

California, and headed east. The U.S. Congress agreed to pay each railroad company for every mile of track it constructed until the two lines met. With this agreement each company raced to build as many miles as it could. The Union Pacific went about hiring thousands of immigrant workers. Most of them came from Ireland, but many also came from Scotland, Germany, and the Scandinavian countries. With plenty of eager immigrant workers, and with less difficult terrain, the Union Pacific line moved steadily west.

The Central Pacific Railroad, on the other hand, was in real trouble. There did not seem to be enough men in the far West willing to do the backbreaking pick and shovel work needed to build a railroad line. Many men were off fighting in the Civil War. Others would start working for the railroad, but soon slipped away to work in the mines. The work was much easier, and the chance of "striking it rich" was too hard to resist.

The Central Pacific bosses grew desperate. The Union Pacific was moving steadily westward, its immigrant work crews constructing as much as 10 miles of track a day. Central Pacific was losing the race across the continent — and the money that went with each mile of track! Where would it find more workers?

Finally, someone made a suggestion: *Why not hire Chinese workers?*

Thousands of Chinese had come to Cali-

91

fornia in the 1850's in search of the "mountain of gold." They had suffered terribly sailing in overcrowded ships. Many of them became ill and died. Those that arrived safely had to work to pay back the people in China who had paid for their passage. The Chinese took on any kind of work. Many of them barely scratched out a living working in gold mines that had been abandoned by others.

Use the Chinese to build the railroad? The Central Pacific bosses thought that the idea was ridiculous. After all, they reasoned, this is tough work. *The Chinese are small and "delicate."* Besides, the bosses added, they are, well, "different." *They eat strange foods, they bathe a lot, and, well, they just do not act like us.* But these were desperate times. One of the bosses finally hired a group of fifty Chinese to haul away some dirt, and do some grading. After each day's work, the boss had to admit that the Chinese workers had done an excellent job. One day he had them do some mason, or stone, work. He was in for another surprise: they worked as well as any crew he had ever watched.

Before long, hundreds, then thousands of Chinese were being hired from northern California, with more coming from China. The Central Pacific needed all the good workers it could get. The terrain, or ground, in the West was more difficult to build on than the ground the Union Pacific covered. The line crossed through deserts and plains, and through high mountains. Huge bridges had to be built, roadbeds leveled, tunnels dug, and paths cut through dense forests.

As the railroad wound around the foothills of the Sierra Nevada, Chinese workmen set about moving tons of dirt to fill the ravines and the valleys. They used only shovels, picks, and wheelbarrows. Where the ravines were too steep, wooden bridges, called trestles, were built. And when the "great army" — for that is what the swarm of Chinese workmen were called — reached the mountains they faced new challenges. Rock cliffs towered fourteen hundred feet high. Nature had left no trails, no ledges, no footholds to cling to. How would the Chinese army overcome this trick of nature?

Centuries before, the ancient Chinese had built high ribbon-like roads on some of China's mountains. Now the workers set about doing the same thing in America. Two or three men were placed in large baskets made from reeds and vines. Four ropes were tied securely to the basket and then, ever so slowly, the men were lowered down from the edge of the cliff. Down and down they went for hundreds of feet — the baskets swaying to and fro in the air — until they reached the place where the railroad roadbed was to be. Here they stopped, and the men began their dangerous work. They chipped holes in the rock face, placed black powder charges inside, then swung away as the charges blasted gaping holes in the rock. In a matter of weeks a roadbed had been blasted out of the rock, but not before some of the Chinese workmen had been blown away or fallen to their death.

More dangers were ahead. The High Sierra's summit rose over 7,000 feet. A 1700 foot tunnel would have to be blasted through the mountain. Nature was ready with more cruel tricks. Biting winter winds came, and a deep snow soon blanketed the mountains. The Chinese workmen built camps under ten to twenty feet of snow. From time to time, an avalanche swept over one of the camps, smothering the workers. When it was time to bring in the locomotives, the Chinese workmen built log sleds, then pulled the locomotives over the mountains.

The United States Congress expected that the transcontinental railroad would be finished about 1876. When newspapers began printing stories in early 1869 that the two railroad companies were drawing close to each other, Americans everywhere grew excited. Newspapers now carried daily accounts of how far each railroad line had gone. The excitement built up and exploded on May 10, 1869. When the gold spike was driven into the ground in Utah, it was the signal for celebrations everywhere.

The engineers and the businessmen of the Central Pacific felt a special pride. So too did the workers. Together, they had planned and built an 1800 mile railroad that crossed plains, deserts and lofty mountains without the use of machinery. The pick, the shovel, the wheelbarrow, the one-horse cart, gunpowder, (and a little nitroglycerine), were all the tools they needed — so long as there were enough willing workers. Of these workers, some 13,000 — four out of five — were Chinese.

Courtesy, Bancroft Library

The pick, the shovel, the wheelbarrow, the one-horse cart, and gunpowder were all the tools they needed.

1869

Writing / Journal Activities

1. The Story

Make up three good questions about the story, "The Men Who Built the Railroad Across America." Write the answers after each question.

2. Find the Headline

Here are three newspaper headlines. Copy the ONE headline that tells the main idea of the story the best.

1. Congress Approves Building Transcontinental Rail Line

2. Union Pacific Building Rail Line to the West

3. Chinese Workers Help Build Transcontinental Rail Line

3. Take It Or Leave It

Here are nine words that might be used to describe a worker today. Copy out the THREE words that best describes the person you would want working for you.

different	happy	young
industrious	punctual	foreign
good looking	old	caring

4. Did He Say That?

Here are six statements. Copy the THREE statements that a Chinese railroad worker might have made.

1. "I still owe money to some people in China."

2. "I came here from Texas."

3. "My hands are blistered from using this jackhammer."

4. "My boss thinks I eat strange food."

5. "My boss hired me because he likes the way I look."

6. "Some of my fellow workers were killed building the railroad."